Successor journal to *Theatre Quarterly* (1971–1981)
VOLUME XIV   PART 4   (NTQ 56)

NOVEMBER 1998

GH00697222

Editors
CLIVE BARKER
SIMON TRUSSLEI

Contents

*New Theatre Quarterly is published in February, May, August, and November by Cambridge University Press, The Edinburgh
Building, Shaftesbury Road, Cambridge CB2 2RU, England*   ISBN 0 521 64850 5   ISSN 0266 – 464X

Editorial Enquiries

Great Robhurst, Woodchurch, Ashford, Kent TN26 3TB, England

Unsolicited manuscripts are considered for publication in *New Theatre Quarterly*. They should be sent to Simon Trussler at the above address, but unless accompanied by a stamped addressed envelope (UK stamp or international reply coupons) return cannot be guaranteed. Contributors should follow the journal's house style as closely as possible. A style sheet is available on request.

Subscriptions

New Theatre Quarterly (ISSN: 0266-464X) is published quarterly by Cambridge University Press, The Edinburgh Building, Shaftesbury Road, Cambridge CB2 2RU, UK, and The Journals Department, 40 West 20th Street, New York, NY 10011-4211, USA.

Four parts form a volume. The subscription price, which includes postage (excluding VAT), of Volume XIV, 1998, is £49.00 (US$85.00 in the USA, Canada and Mexico) for institutions, £28.00 (US$44.00) for individuals ordering direct from the publishers and certifying that the Journal is for their personal use. Single parts cost £13.00 (US$23.00 in the USA, Canada and Mexico) plus postage. EU subscribers (outside the UK) who are not registered for VAT should add VAT at their country's rate. VAT registered subscribers should provide their VAT registration number. Prices include delivery by air. Japanese prices for institutions are available from Kinokuniya Company Ltd., P.O. Box 55, Chitose, Tokyo 156, Japan.

Orders, which must be accompanied by payment, may be sent to a bookseller or to the publishers (in the USA, Canada and Mexico to the North American Branch). Periodicals postage paid at New York, NY, and at additional mailing offices. POSTMASTER: send address changes in the USA, Canada and Mexico to *New Theatre Quarterly*, Cambridge University Press, The Journals Department, 40 West 20th Street, New York, NY 10011-4211.

Claims for missing issues will only be considered if made immediately on receipt of the following issue.

Information on *New Theatre Quarterly* and all other Cambridge journals can be accessed via http://www.cup.cam.ac.uk/ and in North America via http://www.cup.org/.

The Edinburgh Building, Cambridge CB2 2RU, United Kingdom
40 West 20th Street, New York, NY 10011-4211, USA
10 Stamford Road, Oakleigh, Melbourne 3166, Australia

Typeset by Country Setting, Woodchurch, Ashford, Kent TN26 3TB
Printed and bound in the United Kingdom at the University Press, Cambridge

Geraldine Cousin

From Travelling with Footsbarn to 'Wandertheater' with Ton und Kirschen

The first issue of NTQ in February 1985 included a feature on the Footsbarn Travelling Theatre Company which traced the development of the group from its formation in Cornwall in 1971, through its development of a distinctive narrative-based performance style – strong in physicality, visual imagery, and knockabout humour – to its status as an internationally acclaimed company, based now in France but touring extensively in Europe. Geraldine Cousin, the compiler of that feature, provided an update in NTQ33 (February 1993), which focused on Footsbarn's work since 1985, culminating in the 'Mir Caravan' project, in which eight theatre groups toured to the Soviet Union and through Eastern and Western Europe. In May 1992, two members of the group, David Johnston and Margarete Biereye, left to establish a new theatre company in Germany – the *Wandertheater* Ton und Kirschen, now well established, with actors drawn from Germany, France, England, Morocco, Spain, Colombia, Poland, and Australia. Though based in a small German village, Ton und Kirschen has built up its reputation in a number of European countries, and in 1998 was awarded the prize for Performing Arts from the Akademie der Künste, Berlin. Ton und Kirschen is funded partly by the Ministerium für Wissenschaft, and partly by the local district and the town of Potsdam, with a further portion of its income deriving from ticket sales and foreign tours. In December 1997 Margarete and David talked to Geraldine Cousin about their reasons for leaving Footsbarn, and their work with the new company. Geraldine Cousin is Senior Lecturer in Theatre Studies at the University of Warwick, and is author of *Churchill the Playwright* (Methuen), *King John* in the 'Shakespeare in Performance' series (Manchester University Press), and *Women in Dramatic Place and Time* (Routledge). She has recently completed a book for Harwood which documents productions by Sphinx Theatre, Scarlet Theatre, and Foursight Theatre.

COULD *we begin with your reasons for leaving Footsbarn and establishing a new work base in Germany?*

David Really, it was time to go. I joined Footsbarn when I was twenty-five, and I left when I was forty-four. So it was a huge slice of my life. Leaving was a big wrench because Footsbarn was my education, my university. Before Footsbarn, I was just a man on a horse riding in twelve different directions at the same time, and through Footsbarn I found my way to be an actor.

The life we led with Footsbarn, though, and the way things were done had been constructed when we were much younger, and eventually I felt as though I'd outgrown it. I wanted to work on different subjects, with other people, and in a different environment. The work with Footsbarn had been based on

a sort of production method that we'd developed over the years, and then repeated. There was a lot of concentration on producing a product, as quickly as possible, then touring with it for a long time (without really thinking about it again), and then stopping for a bit before producing another product.

Footsbarn had to do this because of the size of the company and the number of people who had to be paid. You have to remember that Footsbarn never received a grant – no sustained help really from anybody. It just existed on what it could earn, and the fees it could get. So, because of the responsibilities the company had, we were forced to become a bit of a theatre factory – though, admittedly, a very successful one.

Margarete I left Germany in 1970 to go to Jacques Lecoq's school in Paris, and after studying there it became clear to me that I didn't want to go back to Germany. I could not see any possibility of creating the kind of theatre I was interested in in Germany, and I didn't want to work in the atmosphere of a state theatre. At Lecoq's I had met English people who, like me, dreamed of a theatre which dispensed with big stages and big cities, and after we left Paris we went together to Cornwall. That was the start of the odyssey with Footsbarn Travelling Theatre – going to rural areas, where people weren't used to theatre, and bringing theatre to the villages, performing out of doors (because this is how one meets people), and then inside, in the halls. If people like what you're doing, they will follow you inside.

Ton und Kirschen began with a similar dream. We wanted to go back to the villages. In 1981 Footsbarn left England to go on the next stage of the odyssey, and it was an incredible experience. The more the years pass by, and the further I look back, the more exraordinary it seems, but after travelling through many countries – continents even – one becomes a little tired of long journeys and continuous changes, and feels a desire to live in calmer circumstances.

In May 1989 Footsbarn travelled from France to Moscow. It took nine days in our bus, and part of the journey was through East Germany. On the motorway we saw signs for Glindow, the village my mother and her family (six generations deep) came from. But in 1989, passing by on the way to Moscow, we weren't allowed to go off the transit road.

We went to Moscow as part of a project called the Mir Caravan. There were eight groups (four western theatre groups and four eastern groups), and we performed first in Moscow and Leningrad, then in Eastern Europe. We wanted to go to East Berlin, but we didn't get permission to perform there, so we performed in West Berlin. At that time the Berlin Wall was still standing, and I remember looking at it with musicians and dancers from Koko, a group from Bukina Faso in West Africa, and they were just amazed. There was this wall! How was it possible? When, soon afterwards, the wall

crumbled, for the first time since I'd left Germany in 1970 I felt a conscious desire to go back. Specifically, I felt a wish to go to Glindow, of which I had really fond memories from my childhood.

As he has already explained, David also wanted to do something away from Footsbarn, and he was entirely in favour of the idea of going to Glindow. Footsbarn was just beginning to rehearse *A Midsummer Night's Dream*, and we let the group know that this would be our last production with them. The *Midsummer Night's Dream* tour was a long one, though, and we didn't actually leave the company until 1992.

In 1991 we performed in Potsdam, which is very close to Glindow, and we put up our performance tent in the middle of Potsdam. When word got around that two members of the company wanted to settle down in Glindow, people were delighted. We also received offers of financial help, and that was extraordinary – people coming to us, not having to knock on doors for support.

We worked with Footsbarn until May 1992. The last performance was in Colombia, where we played at the big international theatre festival in Bogota, and then we travelled on to Cartagena. Our final performance with Footsbarn was in that wonderful exotic place. When David and I got back to Europe we went straight to Glindow, where we had already arranged to meet three other performers who would work with us in the new company.

There was land owned by my family in the village, and we could drive our caravans straight to it. We could live there, and create there. So far we have created six productions with Ton und Kirschen, one each year.

What was the significance of the name you chose for the company?

David Ton und Kirschen means Clay and Cherries. I originally wanted to call the company Bricks and Cherries. In 1991 we visited a pub in Glindow with some friends, and on the wall there was a kind of heraldic shield, with brick factories and cherries on it – representative images of Glindow. Bricks and Cherries doesn't work in German, though, so we decided on Ton und Kirschen.

Margarete Monks discovered clay here in the eleventh century, and they made bricks from it out of which they built a monastery. My grandfather was a brickmaker – and two generations ago there were nine brick factories around the lake of Glindow. Now there's only one remaining factory where bricks are still fired in the old way using a round oven. When I was a child, I used to mould little figures out of the clay, and now Ton und Kirschen use the clay as a basis from which to make masks.

Kirschen means cherries, and there are plenty of cherry trees in our area. In addition to the brickmakers there used to be the *muckers*.

David *Obstmucker* – a local term for fruit growers. They traditionally have small gardens which they work on the side. There are a lot of lakes in the area, and these, along with the sandy soil, are very good for fruit.

What were the major differences between the way you worked with Footsbarn and what you hoped to be able to do with Ton und Kirschen? What hadn't you been able to do with Footsbarn?

David To begin with, the biggest change from Footsbarn was that we didn't have the sort of semi-fiction that it was a collective *mise en scène*, a collective direction. Everything was now in our hands: the administration, the technical side of things, where to find a truck, what subject to do, where to rehearse – everything.

We wanted to work in a different way, from a workshop basis, starting on a subject from an improvisational or 'technique' basis, and to leave the creation of the product until as late in the process as possible. With Footsbarn there was so much physical work to do, around the tent and travelling, that it was usually impossible actually to work on ourselves as actors. The few times we *were* able to do this stick very clearly in my mind as experiences I really enjoyed.

We've now got to the stage with Ton und Kirschen where we can begin the work

Margarete Biereye and David Johnston after a Ton und Kirschen performance at the Lehnin Waldbühne. Photo: Jean-Pierre Estournet.

process for each production with a two-month workshop in which we are able to work on ourselves as actors and also to bring people in to work with us. This is very important for young actors, but I believe it's even more important for middle-aged actors because they tend to get stuck in their own way of doing things. They've got their own tricks, which they wheel out in front of the public, and they need a good kick up the arse now and then from a teacher or an improvisational situation in a teaching workshop where they're suddenly reduced to zero.

The Ton und Kirschen production of *Woyzeck*, with Steve Johnston as the Fool and Margarete Biereye as Marie. Photo: Jean-Pierre Estournet.

We also wanted to work in the local language, in German, which was a big change from Footsbarn where we always performed in English. With Footsbarn, we worked with the knowledge that audiences didn't really understand what we were saying, and so a kind of simplified explicative style was used, with lots of colour and violence and a variety of techniques to explain the basic story. The poetry of the language was a kind of song that went along with this.

I believe that most of your productions to date have been out of doors.

David Yes. The initial idea was to perform in village halls, but we had quickly had to abandon this when we realized that people wouldn't come to the village halls to see something they didn't know about. So we decided to play out of doors, and then we would be able to attract the audiences indoors; but performing outdoors – just in the street, or, preferably, a quiet place – became for us a whole opening up of theatre. We began to look at the *commedia dell'arte*, at

Greek theatre, Shakespearean theatre, all of which were performed out of doors, without lights, with no mystification.

The theatre was just there, in daylight, in sunlight, or in the rain. How did the actors do it? Where did they get their strength from to keep the public watching? Today, it's even more difficult. There are many diversions for the audience, all the time. People can look anywhere. There's no centering. Frequently theatre is played in a sort of black hole, with a light at the end of it, so that it's like watching television – there's nowhere else to look. But outdoors it's exactly the opposite. There's sky, trees, cows, people passing by.

Margarete You don't have the concentration and the silence you get indoors. There is wind blowing, and sometimes traffic noise, and none of these elements must be allowed to distract from the play. So the performance has to be very strong, very physical, very expressive.

David Working out of doors is very important for all actors. I think every actor should

The masked satyrs keeping watch on Thisbe in the Ton und Kirschen *Pyramus and Thisbe*. Performers, left to right: Julie Biereye as Thisbe with Matthew Burton and David Johnston as satyrs. Photo: Jean-Pierre Estournet.

play a *commedia* part, out of doors, on an afternoon in the most impossible situation, without any reliance on effects, just a stage, and a mask. It's the basis of our craft, and we should be encouraged to use it.

Do you use masks a lot for your outdoor performances?

David The mask was developed for out of doors. Its size, its features, its presence: all function out of doors better than our own little faces. You need size out of doors. You can't just be a normal person standing on a stage. The person standing next to a member of the audience is bigger than you are. You need size, and the mask gives you that, along with the costumes. Out of doors, costumes must be grand, bigger than reality.

Nowadays we don't just play in the middle of the street. We look, for example, for woods, or cloisters – special places which have a kind of in-built concentration, so that we don't have to use huge things like drums or people on stilts to gain people's attention. But we still have to be bigger than the sky and the trees, and everything else around us.

Margarete In our last production but one, *Pyramus and Thisbe*, we had two masked choruses, one of maenads and one of satyrs. The masks were very beautiful, and they helped us to capture the spirit of the piece. A mask takes away from a naturalistic way of performing. It allows the actor to travel far.

So the mask has become central to your work?

David For us, the mask is the basic form. The essential part of theatre for us is the actor, and the mask is fundamental, the starting point. I've played with a mask all my life, and I would now find it very difficult to imagine another way of being an actor apart from using masks – masks for research, for construction, for teaching, for learning, for changing, for discovery, for discipline, and for technique.

We've just been to Paris, and there we watched the Noh theatre in which the mask achieves a sublime level of discipline, and, at the same time, a magic quality. The Noh mask itself is open and clear. It doesn't move, it doesn't do anything, but the actor in conjunction with the mask achieves a kind of spiritual being, and there really is no explanation for this.

If you watch Noh theatre, you can't think about the actor who is wearing the mask at all. He disappears completely. Then you watch something on television where you see the actor – who is so busy being wonderful, being a marvellous actor, that you can't see the person he's trying to play. All you can see is the actor.

When you were talking about playing out of doors, David, you spoke about a theatre that was without mystification. Could you say more about this?

David I find that so much in the theatre relies on a kind of mystification, through lights and technical effects, to create within the public an idea that they are watching something important – whereas underneath there is nothing really happening. The mystification is a diversion for the public.

But there is always a secret going on in theatre. The public never know exactly what is happening when they're watching a play, except, perhaps, with agit-prop theatre – but though the ideas expressed in agit-prop theatre may be important and exciting, theatrically it misses something: the secret. It's the secret, for example, of the marionette. The marionette moves around on his own little stage, but the secret is that someone else is pulling the strings. There is a double story going on.

So with Ton und Kirschen we wanted to demystify what we were doing – in other words to make it really simple. And through all our rehearsal stages we try to look at the work and always to ask the same question: how much simpler can it be? How short can a sentence be – a sentence, that is, of movement and gesture? How simply can we tell the story, or express the emotion that is required by the piece?

So often an emotional moment on the stage is drawn out, pulled apart, and the

Top: Steffen Findeisen, David Garlick, and Mohamed El Hassouni as satyrs and Margarete Biereye as a maenad in *Pyramus and Thisbe* (photo: Rolf Schulten). Bottom: Margarete Biereye as Beatrice and David Johnston as Arlecchino in *The Servant of Two Masters* (photo: Jean-Pierre Estournet).

actors chew it and make faces and get further and further into it. Everybody says, 'Bravo! What fine acting that was!', but it's really the actor pulling the audience closer and closer to himself, taking them into his world, rather than the world of the subject or the play. So we try to shorten it all, trim it down, make it as brief as possible, and cut out the sentimentality that the actor is trying to create, or the scene is trying to create. Hamlet's advice to the Players – beginning 'Speak the speech I pray you as I pronounced it to you' – that's the perfect text, the perfect guide for theatre.

When I spoke to you in 1991, when you were still performing A Midsummer Night's Dream *with Footsbarn, you were planning Büchner's* Woyzeck *as your first production.*

Margarete Yes, that was our original intention, but on our visits to Germany, before we had actually founded Ton und Kirschen, we were advised that it was too sombre, too dark a subject, and that we should do something light. So as our first piece we chose something from the *Tales of the Thousand and One Nights* – *Der Bucklige*, or *The Hunchback*.

David We wanted something small and simple that we could play around with, and that was what we used. *Woyzeck* was a play, though, that we'd always wanted to do. It was a subject that was with us.

Margarete We'd lived with the idea of it for a long time. While we were still with Footsbarn we read a lot about Büchner's life and his political engagements. But still, even in our second year in Glindow, people in Germany were advising us against doing *Woyzeck*.

David They said that everyone was tired of it. It's about militarism, and people wanted something else. But we did it anyway, and it was very well received.

Margarete We played it outdoors. We had an old Russian tent, and we called the production *Das astronomische Pferd* (which is

from Büchner's play). We developed the fairground characters, so the fairground people performed the play of *Woyzeck*.

What did you work on after Woyzeck?

Margarete The next production was a *commedia dell'arte* piece, Goldoni's *Der Diener zweier Herren* (*The Servant of Two Masters*). The introduction to *commedia* mask work I'd had with Lecoq had always stayed in my memory, and working outside all the time seemed the ideal situation to do more work of this kind. We bought a trailer and a truck for the Goldoni. The truck held the scenery and costumes, and the trailer housed the seating – benches that beer companies gave us and that we transformed. The seating was raked, like a little amphitheatre, and we had a high stage, since it's very important in *commedia* that the audience see the work of the feet and the legs. Action and words are very closely linked in the Goldoni, and it's all very fast, very physical, very rhythmic.

The next show was *Don Quixote*. This was in 1995, and, as with *Woyzeck*, the desire to work on this had been with us for a long time. We decided to do it in 1995 because there were two actors in the company who were just perfect for the central roles: Matthew Burton for Don Quixote and David Johnston for Sancho. We used the trailer from the previous year, but this time we transformed it into Don Quixote's room. It had two big doors, and at the beginning of the performance these slowly opened so that the audience could look into the room.

The scenery was very heavy to put up and carry around, and when we toured the production to Poland, playing a different venue almost every day for two weeks, we had to put up that heavy set, perform, take it down, and move on to the next place – it was absolutely exhausting. So we got a bit wiser the following year, with our production of *Pyramus and Thisbe*.

We had discovered this story first with Footsbarn when we worked on *A Midsummer Night's Dream*, and this led us to the original in Ovid's *Metamorphoses*. Then in the wintertime, along with organizing the next project,

Scenes from the Ton und Kirschen *Don Quixote*. Top: the Chorus of Actors – Death, the Fool, the Devil, the Angel, and the Queen – with Sancho. Bottom: David Johnston as Sancho, Matthew Burton as Don Quixote, and Georg Lennarz as Rosinante. Photos: Jean-Pierre Estournet.

From the Ton und Kirschen production of *The Cherry Orchard*. Above: the departure scene. Opposite page: Margarete Biereye as Ranyevskaia with David Johnston as Gayev. Photos: Jean-Pierre Estournet.

making applications for financial support, and planning the next tour, David and I give workshops. We do a lot of mask work in these workshops. We use stories as a basis for improvisations, and also to show people how they can adapt a story for performance. We'd worked on the Pyramus and Thisbe story a number of times, and we became very familiar with it. The year after *Don Quixote* we decided to put it on ourselves, but we developed it in a completely different way from the ways we'd approached it before. The older world of the two choruses of maenads and satyrs was interwoven into the whole play.

David The performance took place in an arena situation and was played very simply, against a cloth, with a small stage within a larger playing area. The lovers spoke Latin: so, in a sense, we went back to where we had started with Footsbarn, in that again we were using a foreign language, but we had gone through the process, for five or six years, of speaking the same language as the public.

Using Latin is of course very different from speaking English to non-English audi-

ences, because Latin is a dead language. When I visited Bali, I was very taken by the *wayang* shadow theatre which uses the ancient Javanese language. Working with a language that hasn't been spoken for a long time gives the performer a new kind of freedom to distort the voice and the sound of the text. At the same time there is the problem that the public doesn't know what is being said. I like this contradiction very much and always have done, but with Footsbarn there wasn't really an opportunity to think about it.

Pyramus and Thisbe *was your last production but one, so this brings us to your latest production –* The Cherry Orchard. *Was this also a play that you'd always wanted to work on?*

David *The Cherry Orchard* is a play that has dogged us for years. It's been following us around and we've discussed it many times. It's an impenetrable text when you first read it, boring even, but, like any good play, when you start to delve into it, it suddenly comes alive – with such a richness that it's hard to imagine that any human being could have devised it.

Margarete We'd wanted to do *The Cherry Orchard* for many years, but it never really felt right until this year. We've had the same group of actors now since *Don Quixote*, and we're all quite solid together. Also we could find all the characters in the play within the group.

How did you approach the play?

Margarete For the first time we worked without masks, because with Chekhov it's very important to concentrate on the human aspects. The feelings and relationships and the movements of the soul have to be very subtle: it's not big gesture work. And it was a new approach in another way, because apart from the Latin in *Pyramus and Thisbe* we'd always previously used German – but for *The Cherry Orchard* we used six different languages: German, English, French, Arabic, Polish, and Spanish. With the Goldoni, or *Don Quixote*, or even the Büchner text, it wasn't so difficult for non-German actors to speak in German, but to do a Chekhov text in a language you know only slightly is very difficult. It was a big decision in rehearsals – to use the native language for each actor – but it has worked perfectly.

Despite these innovations, in some ways *The Cherry Orchard* is very much in our style. We do the set-changing between the acts, for example, in front of the audience. There is music accompanying the set changes and the transformations are quite magical. There is a sense of time passing.

David Also we do not ask anybody to believe that the people they're watching on the stage are really the people that they're pretending to be. An important aspect of the way we perform *The Cherry Orchard* is that the public first meet the actors in the auditorium. They are shown to their seats by the actors, who take their coats and sell them drinks or a programme. The actors are actually there in the room, doing everything necessary to prepare for the play. It's all quite open, nothing is concealed, so when the audience see the actors on stage playing characters, they're not asked to believe that

they're really the people they're playing. As Margarete has said, the actors keep appearing throughout the evening to move things around – quite openly.

Cherries feature in the name of your company, and you have mentioned the prevalence of cherry trees around Glindow. Has Chekhov's play any significance for your locality apart from its title?

David *The Cherry Orchard* has considerable relevance to the area where we live. In *The Cherry Orchard* there is the feeling that there is no clear future, and that sense is very strong here too. The whole fabric of society is going through a revolution, and the energy for this comes from western materialism, capitalism, the market place – factors which are changing people's attitudes towards their own cherry orchards, as it were, the lives they had built up within their families. All that is now considered to be of little value. Things must change to fit in with a market economy. So the old gardens are wiped out to build places to sell cars, and so on. The whole fabric of society is changing very fast. People are concentrating on the struggle with the now. The future seems vague and chaotic, and people don't really want to think about that.

What is the composition of your audience?

David   Part of our audience is very family-based. From the beginning, both old and young people came to see the *Wandertheater*. They had seen nothing like it before. There had been no such travelling theatre in the eastern part of Germany for fifty years or more, so it was a completely new experience. The idea of *Wandertheater* had a sentimental side to it: it was something that had been missing, and now it was back again.

Apart from the local elements of the audience, there are the people from Berlin who go out of town for the day and come across Ton und Kirschen. We also get theatre people who are intrigued by an international theatre group based in a small village. Our audience is very varied, very wide, and also very faithful. A lot of people see our shows four or five times.

What are your plans for the coming year?

Margarete   Ton und Kirschen starts at the beginning of March and continues until the end of November each year. That's the cycle. At the beginning of March the group comes together again for training and workshop sessions, and to create the new production. Before they leave for the winter everyone knows what the new production will be, so they can do relevant reading and other kinds of preparation.

This year, 1998, will be the seventh year of Ton und Kirschen, and we have decided not to do a new production, but instead to have a *dimanche*, a Sunday, and carry on working on *The Cherry Orchard*. This production is still very new. We've only played it six times in Glindow and there is a lot of interest in Germany and abroad. People want to see it, and also *Pyramus and Thisbe*, which was a huge success. In 1997 we toured *Pyramus and Thisbe* for three months in France, and we played in Ireland, at the Galway Festival. We had some wonderful reviews of the production in papers from *Le Monde* to *The Irish Times*. The response was huge, and this was really encouraging – a little group from a little village in Germany, about which these overwhelming things were being said.

So we plan to tour again in 1998, but also of course to perform in Glindow. People in our area were very sad because in 1997, for the first time, Ton und Kirschen were away for three months in the summer – though we did rehearse *The Cherry Orchard* in October and then perform it in November.

And the future?

David   I'd like to do a Greek play. I'm very interested in immigration and emigration and refugees, and I'd like to explore this motif within Greek dramatic literature. And we've looked at *The Oresteia* a lot – though I have a real problem with the third part of *The Oresteia*.

There's also Shakespeare, but, for me, Shakespeare has now become more difficult. It's the medieval element within the plays I don't like. Every year, when we're deciding what production to do next, I read a Shakespeare, but I find the medieval thing so far away from what's going on now. Maybe that is not true, I don't know, but the simplicity and the struggle in Greek theatre is much clearer to me at the moment than Shakespeare. I'd like to do Greek theatre, antique theatre. *Pyramus and Thisbe* was a sort of antique theatre, but it wasn't written as a play. Greek theatre is the basis of our theatre, our very roots. And I'd love to do more Chekhov, though I suppose we'll have to wait, having only just done *The Cherry Orchard*. The basic plan is actually to stay where we are and carry on our work.

Juliusz Tyszka

The Orange Alternative: Street Happenings as Social Performance in Poland under Martial Law

Confronted with political opposition, an authoritarian regime predictably responds with force – but also with recognition of a knowable enemy. Confronted with anarchy and laughter, it can be caught wrong-footed – as happened in Poland in the aftermath of Martial Law, when a young surrealist, Waldemar Fydrych, self-designated 'Major', created what he called the Orange Alternative. In a series of published manifestoes and in the street happenings they proclaimed and recorded, the Orange Alternative tickled the soft underbelly of the Jaruzelski regime, and met with responses ranging from hostility to ostensible sympathy to simple bafflement. Juliusz Tyszka here records the progress of a movement and its moving spirit – who, disillusioned with democracy when it came, exiled himself to Paris to invent alternatives anew. Juliusz Tyszka is a past contributor on Polish theatre to NTQ, who teaches in the Institute of Cultural Studies at Adam Mickiewicz University, Poznan.

THE ORANGE ALTERNATIVE, a unique artistic and political phenomenon, was at its prime in the period between Spring 1987 and Autumn 1988. Its manifestations – through happenings – were the common creation of their initiators and animators, but also of the young people of Wrocław, casual passers-by in the centre of the city, and the functionaries of the state militia who were always anxious to participate.

The historical and local background to the Orange Alternative was the period of deep political crisis in Poland, the 'stormy 1980s', going back to the great political break-through of the summer of 1980 – the strikes in Lublin followed by a general strike in the Baltic seaports, and resolved by the agreement between the authorities and strikers, led by Lech Wałęsa, in the Gdańsk shipyard on August 31. The workers were supported and helped by advisors coming from dissident intellectual milieux – the Committee of Defence of Workers, the Flying University, and others – and from Catholic circles.

The Gdańsk agreement included permission for the foundation of independent trade unions, and in the next few days the Solidarity union was founded. Within the first month of its existence it already had ten million members and had become a mass dissident movement. The sixteen months of the 'Solidarity carnival' gave the Polish people an opportunity to act and speak openly in their attempt to build a democratic society.

Although the Communist economic order remained intact, Party officials, continuously pressed by their Soviet comrades, could no longer tolerate the rapid disintegration of the post-Stalinist social and cultural order, and determined that the ten-million-strong social and political movement had to be stopped before it accelerated into revolution. Therefore Martial Law was imposed on the Polish people on 13 December 1981, and was duly announced on TV by General Wojciech Jaruzelski, the party leader, prime minister, and commander-in-chief of the army.

The imposition of Martial Law was in fact a *coup d'état* performed by the wing of the Communist Party controlled by Jaruzelski and, above all, by the Polish army, who took control of all institutions and gave the order to arrest all important Solidarity activists, including the president, Lech Wałęsa.

Martial Law was suspended on 31 December 1982 and called off on 22 July 1983, the National Holiday of People's Poland, but many regulations imposed on 13 December 1981 remained in force until the fall of the Communist regime in the Spring of 1989.

All political, artistic, scientific, regional, social, cultural, and student associations and institutions, as well as trade unions, were suspended, including Solidarity, of course. The movement was officially dissolved in October 1982, after the refusal of a great many of Solidarity's leaders to collaborate with the Martial Law regime. The censors started to act, in an attempt to repudiate the concessions of the 'Solidarity carnival'.

After a hard struggle which cost a few dozen people their lives, the activity of the Polish dissidents diminished in 1984–85. People were tired of constant fighting, and the now clandestine Solidarity appeared to have lost 'Jaruzelski's war'. Party propaganda triumphantly announced the coming of 'normalization'.

In 1986–87 political, economic, and moral stagnation reached its peak. The Communist powers seemed strong enough to survive for decades, surrounded by the hate of a passive nation – for *perestroika* in the Soviet Union changed neither the attitude of the Polish people towards the Communist authorities and the USSR, nor the tough regulations of Martial Law which were still in force.

Emergence of the Movement

However, the attitude of the Communists started to change. The isolation of the Polish authorities, deepened by the tough attitude of the West (with the Polish government owing western banks more than 30 billion dollars), became obvious, and the Communists began to realize that it was impossible to exercise absolute power against a passive but openly hostile nation and western creditors without the strong support of their Soviet allies, who were weakened by the defeat in Afghanistan and by *perestroika*. The state militia and ominous riot militia forces (ZOMO) gradually became more indulgent, as did the censors, courts, and state administration. The field of action was ready for the coming of the Orange Alternative.

The movement, led by Waldemar Fydrych (nicknamed Major), appeared in the city of Wrocław. It was appropriate that this city – formerly the German Breslau – should have given birth to such an original attitude and activity. The greatest 'melting pot' of nations and cultures in Poland, its population in the 1950s consisted mostly of those who just after the Second World War had been displaced from the former Polish territories of Western Ukraine, Belorussia, and Lithuania into the former German territories of Lower Silesia.

In the 1970s Wrocław became a vibrant cultural centre, deeply touched and changed by the creation of the Polish Laboratory Theatre of Jerzy Grotowski, the State Pantomime Theatre of Henryk Tomaszewski, the State Polish Theatre of Jerzy Grzegorzewski, the State Contemporary Theatre of Kazimierz Braun, the creations of another famous theatre director Helmut Kajzar, the great International Festival of Open Theatre which was inaugurated in 1967, the presence of the great poet-plawright, Tadeusz Rózewicz, the activity of the monthly *Odra*, and a whole milieu of fine artists.

In the 1980s Wrocław, along with Gdańsk, was the most powerful centre of resistance against Communist power. In 1982 and 1983 tens of thousands of its inhabitants regularly participated in mass demonstrations and in street fights with riot militia. The clandestine Solidarity with its legendary regional leaders, Władysław Frasyniuk and Józef Pinior, had some of its strongest support here.

The leader of the Orange Alternative, Waldemar Fydrych-Major, was born in 1953, and graduated from Wrocław University in the Departments of History and History of Art. He took his present nickname in the 1970s, when he was pretending to be mentally handicapped in order to avoid doing compulsory military service after his studies. During one of his sessions with a psychiatrist, Fydrych promoted the doctor to the rank of colonel and made himself a major. 'Then, when I had gone to the psychotherapeutic camp', recalls Fydrych, 'and led the military manoeuvres there, I became Major for good.'[1]

In April 1981, during the period of the 'Solidarity carnival', Major was one of the organizers of the Wrocław Peace March, the only one in the Soviet-dominated bloc. He was also an activist of the Movement for New Culture, the only student organization in Poland with no strictly political programme – its founders intending to promote a new paradigm of culture rather than Solidarity's idea of revolution.

The MNC became the forum of artistic opposition for Wrocław students and young intelligentsia, drawing inspiration from the anarchistic aspects of the western counterculture of the 1960s, but the intention of its founders was to expand its influence among workers and clerks.

In October 1981 the MNC organized a demonstration in the very centre of Wrocław, bearing banners proclaiming: 'Down with Symmetry!' and 'Long Live Free Imagination'. A street demonstration was in itself something unusual at that time, and the content of the slogans deepened the surrealistic effect. As Fydrych later declared: 'People were associating this peculiar demonstration rather with happenings and street art than with real social problems' (p. 21).

Major was the editor of the movement's ephemeral periodical, *Orange Alternative*. For the choice of colour the editors gave various explanations: orange is a mixture of red and yellow, the colour of an orange (oranges, as well as all exotic fruits, were almost impossible to buy in Poland at the time), and the colour of the rising sun which in India and China is a symbol of wisdom.

In *Orange Alternative* Fydrych and his colleagues from MNC published surrealistic long short stories, as well as slogans, manifestos, and texts by Krishnamurti, and André Breton's well-known letter to the rectors of European universities. The most original and most popular slogan of that time was: 'Proletarians – Be Beautiful!'

The First Street Happenings

In autumn 1981, during a long strike of Polish academies – one of the thousands organized in the period of the 'Solidarity carnival' – Major arranged his first street happening. Every night the militia would take away posters left on the university walls by striking students. One night the student unit led by Major left the building and sang the Polish birthday and name-day song, 'Live for a Hundred Years', to the men of the militia. The following night they sang 'The Internationale', and a few hundred photographs were taken as documentation of the action. The militia withdrew, leaving the walls untouched.

'We named the building of the Faculty of Philosophy *Fort No. 1*', recalls Fydrych, 'organizing the work of our revolutionary staff and editing our periodical there. In *Orange Alternative* we were writing mostly about art but at that time it was first and foremost a political art' (p. 8).

Gradually Major's ideas began to focus on the concept of 'socialist surrealism'. 'Everything is moving within deep feelings of surrealist imagination', he wrote in the first issue of *Orange Alternative*. 'Socialism is good for fragmentary people who acquire a certain perfection in the lack of totality. Nothing can define it except for the magic of routine in the office. . . . Freedom is a comfort' (p. 103–4).

In the third issue of *Orange Alternative* Major published 'The Decree on Setting Up the Council of Commissars of Orange Revolution in the Wrocław Academy of Fine Arts' – its first proclamation that schizophrenia is 'the highest quality jolt', as 'reality is the oldest and most dangerous enemy of a man'. Other slogans included 'Down with intellectual art!' and 'Long live socialism, the object of comic-strip art of the highest quality!' (p. 108).

Finally Fydrych announced the 'Manifesto of socialist surealism':

Everybody knows that the poetry of Salvador Dali's paintings contains more surrealism than the great poems of Karl Marx. Even novels by Lenin are not equal to these paintings. . . .
   It is worth knowing if the cancer of rationalism has devoured your brain or not. . . . Kill reason. . . . There is no other way of returning to nature. Isn't it the height of happiness to be a mechanism of the great cosmic machine? I recommend it. . . .

The world cannot exist at long range without surrealism. But why have young people been drowned in the ether of boring blankness? Who does it? This gloomy theatre, so called THOUGHT. The guilty are who? First and foremost the existentialists. . . . Philosophers are also guilty. . . . Who else is exhorting us to hold politicians in contempt? Politicians are great. Philosophers are finished. Politicians have always been surrealists. Let's love politicians. . . . It has been difficult for pure rationalism to conquer public toilets. Surrealism has survived there thanks to politicians. Where else may we observe such a strict connection between relief and aesthetic experience? . . . Who among philosophers, I am asking seriously, would be so courageous as to announce: *I am happy, therefore I exist* instead of: *I am thinking, therefore I exist*?

Do not read Dostoievski. The world is represented better in press-cuttings. This is a work for every beginner in surrealism. . . .

The times of socialism are particularly advantagous for the development of art. It is important that every day an ordinary man gets to know more, feels better, and that the reality is growing. And the importance of ordinary man's existence in socialism is based on permanent surrealist transformations. . . . Nowadays the impetus of social life has overcome the boldest dreams of the surrealists from the 1920s and 1930s. . . .

The only solution for the future and for today is surrealism. . . . After all, the whole world is a work of art. Even a single militia man on the street is an object of art. Let's play, our fate is not tragic. There is no sense in suffering since we may be happy (p. 9–11).

Such exhortations could hardly be tolerated by the leaders of the student strike at Wrocław University, involved in 'serious' political struggle with the Communists. They imposed censorship on *Orange Alternative*. Major and his colleagues moved their headquarters to the Academy of Fine Arts, which in November and December 1981 began to be a truly creative and open free school of art.

In his public activity during the 'Solidarity carnival' Major always stressed the need for a total reconstruction of young people's minds. He was deeply convinced that the organizational structures created by Solidarity were not revolutionary enough to cause a genuine change of mentality and sensitivity in young Poles. His concepts and way of life, as well as the ideas of the Movement for New Culture, were trans-cending the limits of hard political struggle imposed on dissident movements by the Communists.

The Goals of 'Surrealistic Revolution'

The goals of his 'surrealistic revolution' were free creation, irony, lightness, happiness, and amusement in human existence, all hard to achieve in any contemporary society – and quite impossible to achieve in Poland at the end of 1981, when Martial Law was declared, strikes were bloodily crushed by the militia and the army, and all democratic concessions withdrawn. Fydrych joined 'ordinary' street fights not only in Wrocław but also in Warsaw where, being after all 'an army professional', he became the leader of a punks' unit.

Soon he became bored with the banality of street rioting and returned to surrealist activities. His first famous action in 1982 was painting joyful dwarfs on the walls of several Polish cities. The walls were covered with anti-Communist slogans and Solidarity symbols, whose authors were being chased by police and severly punished. Major and his friend nicknamed 'Pablo' were detained several times in different cities. In Katowice, after six hours of very surrealistic interrogation, the police officer agreed to treat their action as 'juvenile fancy'. In Świnoujście they were forced to write an official declaration that a dwarf was an apolitical symbol.

In the summer of 1982 a few activists of clandestine Solidarity used Fydrych's home as a hiding-place. When the secret police began surveillance, Major took counter-offensive measures, which are considered his second serious artistic action in the period of Martial Law, by posting the announcement, 'Washing machine for sale, small, made in Yugoslavia', on the walls of his district. In that era of severe market shortages such a product was sheer luxury, and in the following days Major's place was visited by several dozen people and to the police seemed to be the centre of a great dissident movement.

The last of Fydrych's artistic initiatives in 1982 was his application for a passport,

The dwarfs and the crowd during the Orange Alternative's 'Celebration of Children's Day', 1 June 1987.

travel documents then being conferred on citizens of the Polish People's Republic by regional militia headquarters. He expressed his wish to go to Jamaica in order to join the Rastafarian movement, declaring:

I will always be free. My decision is in harmony with the basic interests of the Polish People's Republic and also with the interests of all mankind. I know that, being an anarchist, aiming to free society from the chains of a bureaucratic state, I am danger No. 1 for every state power. Therefore my will to leave is highly understandable. I think neither the state, nor I, can let such an opportunity slip by.
At the same time I wish all the best to the people who will have to deal with my application (p. 96).

The 'Manifesto of Socialist Surrealism' was appended to the application. Fortunately for the history of Polish contemporary art, the militia did not award Fydrych the precious document.

In the following years Major developed and fine-tuned his strategy of street happenings. He undertook many trials on a smaller scale in 1986. The first big event, enabling him to define his own model of street events, was the happening on the occasion of April Fools' Day 1987, when a few dozen students demonstrated their joy with aluminium pots on their heads and forks in their hands. The militia units, taken completely by surprise, took more than an hour to launch their attack.

Major closes his own surrealist description of the event with irony: 'Militia men of this ancient Polish city showed a full understanding of contemporary art and acted with invention, making a great contribution to the cultural development of the capital of Lower Silesia' (p. 45).

The Visit of the Kindly Dwarfs

The next happening, held on the occasion of Children's Day, 1 June 1987, was much bigger and better organized. Some days beforehand, posters and leaflets (soon collected up fervently by the militia) announced to the citizens of Wrocław that they would be visited by a few hundred kindly dwarfs. 'The dwarf has played a great role in the history of the world', wrote Major in the leaflet:

Today we cannot say for sure that we are dealing with mammals. Neither *Encyclopedia Britannica* nor *The Short History of the Russian Communist Party* (*Bolsheviks*) or other great sources of knowledge in the world say anything about them. The only people who have met them are Snow White, Little Orphan Marysia, and the Brothers Grimm. . . .

Socialism has fully acknowledged the idea of dwarfs. As early as the Great October Revolution part of the Red Army (the units of Budenny's cavalry in particular) were disguised in red hats, and many soldiers, thanks to the new ideology, started to believe they were dwarfs. In the Polish People's Republic red hats appear frequently. They will be seen in Wrocław, on Świdnicka Street, near the clock at 3 p.m. on 1 June. A dwarf can turn out to be a great patron and friend of economic reform in Poland. Some people even say it can be its consequence.

Come! You are not worse than Snow White and Little Orphan Marysia. . . . Long life to surrealism! Let the world forces of peace flourish in the shadow of martial art. . . .

P.S. Do not be surprised that some dwarfs, which will appear on Świdnicka, will be of Gulliver's size. This strange mutation is a result of an explosion in a certain nuclear power station. The heavy isotopes coming from there have been absorbed by small mushrooms and forest undergrowth – dwarf's delicacy (p. 47).

The principal characters of the event were: dwarfs (young people with red hats on their heads) giving away sweets and candies; a teddy-bear; some characters from the most popular fairy-tales; and, of course, great Gulliver-sized dwarfs – riot militia men.

The scenario was easy to foresee: Świdnicka Street near the street clock and Old Market Square were carefully watched by the secret Security Service from early on the night before. Then, after the clock showed 3 p.m., whoever was wearing a red hat (not including the great teddy-bear in the dark glasses which were favoured also by General Jaruzelski, or Puss in Boots) or was found to be giving away sweets or greeting children was immediately arrested.

'It was a meeting of International Children's Day with the International Communist Movement', wrote Major afterwards in his surrealist report. 'Finally the Security Service had an opportunity to show its interest in something more colourful than a shadowy Underground. The fight with the Underground changes them into badgers, whereas here, instead of underground passages and holes, it is enough to stay in daylight and wait for the effects.'

Dwarfs are dancing, the pageant, moving like a snake, is mixing with two militia cars. Some dwarfs are knocking on doors and greeting people inside. They shout: 'Dwarfs do exist in this world!' . . . The militia men expertly approach them, embrace their arms. Two hats in a tango: one blue and one red. . . .

Suddenly a rumble! Everyone freezes. Guns or tear-gas? Nobody moves.

Somebody has shot a bag emptied of sweets. Now he is laughing and shoots another one. . . . The mob fills all of Świdnicka Street. So this is Revolution! . . .

The militia turns on loud-speakers: 'Dismiss! Take off red hats! Papers of all people who do not take hat off will be checked!' . . .

'Mummy, why do they arrest dwarfs?'

'They exist in capitalism and do not exist in socialism.'

'The show is finished!' say loudspeakers.

Shouts: 'Children's Day, the show is still on!' . . .

The militia headquarters on Lakowa Street. A functionary raises his voice: 'Even happenings have their limits.'

The subject of the interrogation expresses his opinion that the functionary is not a connoisseur of contemporary art, the latter shouts that he has seen many happenings. Manly discussion, very difficult.

'Who organized it?' – a question.

'What was the supposed course of the event?'

'Everyone was supposed to invent something funny.'

'What have you invented?'

'Pills of happiness.'

The pills are taken out of the rucksack.

'What are they exactly, these pills of happiness?'. The watchfulness of the functionary has grown.

'They are pills of happiness.'

One of the functionaries tastes them and says they are peppermints.

'Listen, man, do you really believe you will be happy after eating this?' shouts the interrogator with compassion in his voice. . . .

The sound of a guitar can be heard in the headquarters club-room, where the dwarfs are waiting for conversations. The Children's Day celebration goes on. Everyone has already eaten lots of pills of happiness.

'Who will clean the papers off the floor?' asks a functionary in the club-room.

Invisible hands move and the papers disappear.

'Now I believe in dwarfs', says the functionary in the interrogation room' (p. 47-50).

The strategy invented and applied by Major and his friends was by now clear: to show the surrealistic quality of 'socialist democracy' under Soviet domination.

Absurdity in Confrontation with Fear

It was known both to Major and to the state authorities that every street demonstration had to have the state's authorization. Everyone knew the fate of the organizers and the participants in the demonstration against the Iranian occupation of the American Embassy in Teheran, held by the illegal Confederation for Free Poland in 1979 at the entrance of the Iranian Embassy in Warsaw: they were arrested and held for 48 hours, and the detentions were followed by long periods of surveillance. Unauthorized celebrations, even as innocent as the one in Wrocław, had to service the power of the state or be deemed hostile to the regime.

Major and his colleagues called themselves Orange Alternative to commemorate their beginnings in the roles of surrealists. Their happenings were a mixture of art, children's play and political manifestation. They were also an intensification of the everyday surrealism of Polish reality in the 1980s, since our life, subordinated to the 'spirit of togetherness', contained plenty of absurdity.

But probably the most important function of Fydrych's happenings was therapeutic. The events on Świdnicka Street, Old Market Square, and their surroundings enabled the participants to overcome their fear – the most important and the most ominous effect of Communist power, especially during the period of Martial Law. After hundreds of bloody street fights all over Poland (and in Wrocław in particular). it was not easy to face once more the militia on the street, to be arrested and interrogated. It was possible, however, and it turned out that the police were not as tough, severe, and cruel as they

had been before. The times had changed, the powers seemed not to be as omnipotent as in 1982–83.

The year 1987 was rich in Orange Alternative activities. After the celebration of Children's Day the inhabitants of Świdnicka Street, the Security Service and militia experienced several stormy events – a demonstration against heat on 1 August; a happening on 1 September, the International Day of Peace; one month later a happening to commemorate toilet paper (shortages of toilet paper having been a cause of distress to Poles through almost fifty years of communist rule, only to disappear in 1989 with the collapse of Communism); the celebration of the Day of the Militia (7 October); the celebration of the Day of the Polish People's Army (12 October); the ceremonial funeral of toilet paper (15 October); the Eve of the Seventieth Anniversary of the Great October Revolution (6 November); a happening on the occasion of the National Referendum for Economic Reform (27 November); and finally a celebration for St. Nicholas's Day (7 December).

Surrealism versus Subrealism

In each of these events artistic and political aspects were inseparable. Major himself commented on his artistic intentions:

After the demonstration on 1 October, commemorating toilet paper, a militia man interrogating Major says: 'Do you know that it was an attempt to change the social and political system in our country?' Fydrych answers: 'I appeared on Świdnicka Street in a paper sack and with the stocking on my head because I was creating art there. . . . I am creating dialectical art, influencing people's consciousness. I think everything is art, everything is an object of art.'

The interrogation is finished. . . . A Security Service agent, who is quitting the building, confides to a colleague that he is going out into the city to create dialectical art (p. 58).

In his description of the happening on the occasion of the National Referendum on 27 November, Major writes:

'The dialectic of the Polish street is a constant clash between surrealism and subrealism. . . . The government of the Polish People's Republic, the avant-garde of world surrealism, proposes to the people a little hocus-pocus, the event is entitled *Referendum* or the hours of great sincerity. . . . It is a happening – folly, great proposition with no way to refuse it. . . . Ha, ha, hi, hi, surrealism or dadaism? The pictures of this event resemble that famous work by Rembrandt, *Night Watch*. . . .

The militia men commit an error and arrest Security Service agents. . . . The scenes from Brueghel and Rembrandt give way to the open theatre. Logic is unnecessary. Let's devote ourselves to the beautiful cause of overcoming the social system in happening (p. 70–1).

Of course, Fydrych was perfectly aware of the political dimension of his actions. In his commentary on the Peace Day happening of 1 September he says:

An independent anti-fascist demonstration is not possible in this country. It is forbidden here to organize anything which has not got the approval of the authorities. Even an independent fight against AIDS would be treated as an attempt to change the political system.

It is a funny situation when they arrest people who demonstrate against fascism. When you are finally arrested you watch the legal anti-fascist manifestation on the TV in the militia head-quarters and you see what kind of hypocrisy all that official *blah, blah, blah* about peace is. . . .

I wanted to show this by organizing this demonstration (p. 54).

In the surrealist report from the celebration of St. Nicholas's Day, Major wrote openly: 'The struggle with the state of torpor and separation, the struggle for the victory of unselfishness, the aspiration for the smile, breaking sad alienation, all this pushed the united forces of good and joy into action' (p. 72-3).

The reactions of the Communist powers were serious – and revealed fear. In spite of the joyful, carnival-like atmosphere at the festivities of Orange Alternative, the young participants were being arrested, detained, interrogated, sometimes humiliated and beaten by the riot police.

The most spectacular event in 1987 was the celebration of the Eve of the Seventieth Anniversary of the Great Socialist October Revolution on 6 November. In the procla-mation printed in the leaflet Major wrote:

Comrades! It is high time to break the passive attitude of the working class. Let's begin to celebrate the Eve of the Great October Revolution. Let's gather as early as 6 November, at Świdnicka Street, at 4 p.m. under 'the clock of history'.

Comrades! Put on red clothes. If you do not have any red clothes ask your neighbour to lend you her red bag. If you have got nothing red you may buy a baguette with ketchup. If you do not have a red flag, paint your nails red. . . .

THE IDEA OF LENIN AND TROTSKY IS ETERNAL!

The Council of Peoples' Commissars.

P.S. Come along with your dog, we will organize a gala of dogs under the title *Dogs on the Head of Revolution*. . . .

BOW WOW!

The celebration will conclude in the bar, *Barbara*, where the participants of this public meeting will eat . . . red borsch, the typical Polish Christmas Eve soup, and other appropriate dishes (p. 66).

Major begins his surrealist report of the celebration with an analysis of Leninism:

Leninism starts in the Moscow Mausoleum and finishes in the people's hearts. Exceptionally long queues in front of butchers' shops are the redoubt of Communism. Leninism is a constant waiting for better times. . . .

The battleship *Potemkin*, the spirit of dialectical materialism, was supposed to appear first, then the cruiser *Aurore*, and the great *mise en scène*: the attack on the Winter Palace. Finally there were carolers with a great red star and the great march of the Red Cavalry. The role of the Winter Palace was in that case played by bar *Barbara* (p. 65–6).

As on many other occasions, Major and his assistants moved out of their homes a few days before 6 November to avoid 'premature arrest'. Then, as Wojciech Marchlewski writes in his 'Chronicle of Events' published in the monthly *Dialog*:

On the morning of 6 November, thousands of leaflets are given away to the passers by in the centre of Wrocław –

People are laughing and promise to come. Around 11 a.m. 'the propaganda unit' glue a dozen posters on the walls near Świdnicka Street. Around midday the first militia patrols appear, checking the papers of all young people, paying particular attention to people with big bags, rucksacks, etc. . . . Later the first militia cars appear. They block the Old Market Square and passages. . . . A few cars stop in front of bar *Barbara*. . . .

Around 3 p.m. the barmaid from *Barbara* hangs a piece of paper on the door. The inscription says: 'Closed due to a malfunction'. At 3.30 p.m. the

Orange Alternative's 'Celebration of the Eve of the Seventieth Anniversary of the Great October Revolution', 6 November 1987. The inscription on the banner (top photo) reads: 'Do not divorce our neighbours from the East.'

mob at Świdnicka is already dense. . . . The functionaries advise the people to quit the place for their own safety.

In the sports store *Stadion* the crew of the battleship *Potemkin* start preparations for their show. Four cartons will play the role of the battleship's sides. . . . At the same moment the crew of the cruiser *Aurore* gathers on the opposite side of the street, in the shop *Merkury*. There are a lot of secret police agents inside. . . . A young pregnant girl enters the shop and goes into one of the fitting-rooms. The crew follows her. They paint their faces red, and one of them puts a mask of Lenin on his face. The belly of the 'pregnant' girl turns into a strip of tarpaulin with holes for the crew's heads. . . .

The unit of Revolutionary Infantry gathers in the *Feniks* store on the Old Market Square. They have put on red sport tracksuits and are carefully checking the sports equipment in stock.

A few hundred meters from there is a bus stop where the Proletarians are coming to take part in the Revolution. (They are genuine workers, members of local clandestine Solidarity units from the great Wrocław factories, Polar and Dolmel). Under their coats they hide red shirts and a red banner.

The churchyard at King Casimir the Great Street is the gathering point of the Red Cavalry. . . . A girl liaison officer comes along and brings Budenny hats. Some other liaison officers bring wooden or cardboard horses and wooden guns. Two people bring an original red banner with the inscription 'The Anniversary of the Great Socialist October Revolution'.

The Angel of the Revolution finally comes. His friends help him disguise himself. They decorate his arms with great red wings and put a long white night-dress on him. They put a halo on his head.

Nearby, beside the Monopol hotel, the carolers gather. They put the great red star on a long stick and develop the banner with the inscription 'Red Borsch'.

At 4 p.m., according to plan, the battleship *Potemkin* appears on Świdnicka Street coming out of the shop *Stadion*. The militia men jump on its crew of four, tear the cartoon ship-sides, and after several minutes of fighting arrest the revolutionary sailors. Hundreds of people rush to see what is going on.

At 4.05 p.m. the cruiser *Aurore* with its crew of seven people appears on Świdnicka and tries to reach the clock. Militia men attack them. The crowd shouts: 'Revolution! Revolution!' Some people blow whistles. The militia men are nervous. The crew sits on the asphalt. The functionaries arrest them. People from the crowd take the places of *Aurore*'s crew. Struggle goes on. New people are arrested. A few militia cars are already filled with young revolutionaries.

At 4.10 p.m. the revolutionary infantry in red tracksuits appears on Old Market Square. They blow their whistles. The entrance to Świdnicka Street is blocked by militia. Only the commander of the infantry forces his way through the row of militia men.

Suddenly an African man in a red cap appears on Świdnicka Street. Everyone looks at him as if he were a ghost. He disappears in one of the little streets.

At the same time the Proletarians arrive by bus at the stop facing the bar *Barbara*. They wear red shirts with the inscription 'I will be working more'. Their banners say: 'We demand the rehabilitation of Lev Trotsky', 'We demand the return of Comrade Yeltsin to Moscow' (Yeltsin having at the time been driven from the capital by Gorbachev), and finally: 'We demand eight-hour working days for the militia.' The Proletarians are arrested at the corner of Świdnicka Street.

At 4.20 p.m. the carolers appear. They carry a long stick with a red star on top and a banner with the slogan 'Red Borsch'. The one carrying the stick is arrested.

Budenny's cavalry attacks from an underground passage on Świdnicka. Militia men wait for them. They break and tear their wooden and cardboard horses, and destroy their wooden guns.

The Angel of the Revolution now enters the shambles. He cannot force his way through the dense crowd. He turns and goes up to the fast-food kiosk. The lady in the kiosk hangs a piece of paper announcing: 'Closed'. No bread-rolls. The Angel leans forward and asks her to give him two portions of ketchup on his hand. The Angel is arrested. . . .

Several members of the dispersed unit of Cavalry gather in front of bar *Barbara*. At 5 p.m. the bar is open again. A Security Service agent asks the barmaid if there is red borsch on the menu. She denies it.

The revolutionaries enter the bar and occupy one of the tables. They order four bottles of strawberry juice, put on their revolutionary caps, and drink. Militia men arrest the cavalry. A female customer comes up and says: 'Boys, you have been wonderful.' The commander salutes and answers: 'Thank you in the name of the Revolution.' The customers in the bar applaud.

Those arrested totalled 150, some of whom are casual passers-by who happened to be wearing something red. The crowd fills the club-room of the militia headquarters on Łąkowa Street. The transmission of the Moscow celebration of the Great October Revolution comes on TV. People applaud the speeches of Soviet leaders and sing *The Internationale*. Militia men try to silence them without any result. One of the revolutionaries paints a slogan on a red flag, a fragment of the club-room's decoration. A militia man bursts into the room, takes the flag from the wall, and tramples it. The revolutionaries applaud him.

After the interrogation the revolutionaries are set free. They wait for their comrades outside. They greet the guardians of the headquarters. The response is warm and friendly.[2]

In December Waldemar Fydrych and his Orange Alternative were awarded an artistic prize by clandestine Solidarity.

The activity of Major's movement in 1988 began with the happening-celebration of the end of carnival on 17 February. The event was carefully watched by the authorities, who finally seemed to be taking the movement of young 'happeners' more seriously, and were considering alternative reactions to its stormy development. The crowds on Świdnicka were becoming too large and an official stand had to be taken.

One of the party propaganda workers published a surrealistic political analysis of Orange Alternative's activities. 'They have adopted an infantile method', he wrote, 'to hide their true intention. . . . In the Orange movement we may discover the embryo of a political power able to destroy our political system.'[3]

The next happening was organized for 1 March, which Major proclaimed to be the Day of the Functionary of the Secret Service. Then Fydrych and his friends appeared on Świdnicka Street on 8 March to celebrate International Women's Day, other demonstrations being held on that occasion by Orange Alternative branches in Gdańsk and Poznań.

'Free Major'

The militia arrested Major on that day, and on the following day he was sentenced to sixty days imprisonment for 'disturbing public order'. Soon the walls of Wrocław were covered with pictures of crying dwarfs and the inscriptions 'Free Major'. Forty eminent Polish intellectuals wrote an open letter to the Communist authorities demanding Fydrych's release. Even the members of the official student union from Wrocław University wrote in protest.

On 21 March happenings celebrating the first day of Spring took place not only in Wrocław but also in Warsaw, Cracow, Gdańsk and Poznań. On Świdnicka Street five thousand people celebrated the drowning of the puppet in dark glasses which symbolized not only the passing of Winter but also of General Jaruzelski.

The event in Wrocław was watched by a spokesman of the Minister of Internal Affairs, Major Wojciech Garstka, who afterwards appeared to display an indulgent attitude. He stated that in spite of the fact that the meeting was illegal, the militia let the young people 'sow their wild oats freely'.

Except for a few cases I did not see any aggression. The only people hostile to the militia were the older ones who were aggressively encouraging young people to fight with militia men

He expressed his admiration for the young functionaries 'who stayed cool in many hot situations', and finally gave the diagnosis:

What I saw was a crowd and public fun. Let's presume these young people are seeking only a serious discussion, not a row. Maybe they care about some serious problems, e.g., trying to define themselves and find themselves in adult life. It would be worth hearing such a message.

I would be interested in helping them to define themselves as citizens who could think critically.

On the other hand there were several publications which were openly hostile to Major and his movement. In a letter to the editor of a party journal from Wrocław, *Gazeta Robotnicza*, an 'anonymous reader' described Fydrych as 'an anarchist who misleads young people', and asked the authorities how long they would tolerate his activities. Questions raised about his unemployment – a grave sin in a Communist state – unregistered residence, and evasion of military service sounded ominous. The letter was an open threat on the part of the secret police.

Fydrych was in prison, but his movement was expanding rapidly, and the Communist authorities were undecided whether to adopt a soft or a tough attitude. The situation was very different from that of 1982. Strikes, street fights, and bloodshed were impossible. The riots would prove that the Communists were able to maintain their power only by using force. All the terror, all the military and bureaucratic effort of the 1980s would have been in vain. So the Communists eventually decided to tolerate Major, his movement, and their 'public fun'. Fydrych was tried once more on 29 March, and was acquitted.

The next happening took place on 1 June, International Children's Day. For the first time the militia did not react even when one of their cars was rocked and painted. Security Service agents limited their activity to filming and taking pictures. And by now the situation in the country was starting to change. In May 1988 several strikes took place in different Polish factories and as usual Wrocław was one of the centres of the Solidarity revival.

On 27 June the leaders of the strike, Czesław Borowczyk and Józef Pinior, were due to be tried in one of the Wrocław courts. The trial eventually took place one week later, and both activists, when released from prison, were able to take part in the happening organized in their support. Inscriptions on banners read: 'Free Borowczyk and Pinior', 'Join Wrocław to Armenia', 'Where is the Militia?' Participants carried portraits of Marx, Engels, Lenin, and Pinior, and Major read his surrealist poem on Lenin, socialism, and eroticism. There were no militia around. The event ended in Old Market Square.

On 19 August Major organized a happening in the Karkonosze Mountains, on the Polish-Czechoslovak border, to commemorate the 'brotherly help' of the Warsaw Pact to the Czechoslovakian people in 1968. On the peak of Śniezka Polish forces were supposed to meet their Czech counterparts and to celebrate the anniversary together. Major wrote in the leaflet:

We are anxious about the fate of our friends. Where is Comrade Husak . . . , what happened to Comrade Strougal? Now, twenty years after our help, anti-socialist forces endanger our Great Cause again. Do not let things go their own way, let's repeat this terrific action on its twentieth anniversary. Let's cross the Czechoslovakian border at different points, let the slogan 'Brotherly Help is Eternal' guide us. Let's arm ourselves in plastic and cardboard tanks. We will demonstrate socialism with a human face.

Unfortunately the Polish forces were arrested long before they reached the frontier. Only a small Czech unit reached the fixed meeting point, where Major, disguised in a *samurai* costume, was arrested by a border patrol, taken to a watch-tower post, and interrogated by the commander, a Colonel. 'Let's speak Pole to Pole', began the Colonel.

'First and foremost let's talk soldier to soldier', Major replied. Then he stated that he was a prisoner of war protected by the Hague Convention. The Colonel anwered that Major had taken all the military responsibility for the effects of his action. They addressed each other as 'Colonel' and 'Major'.

The happening in the Karkonosze Mountains was the last important event organized by Orange Alternative. The political situation in Poland began to change rapidly. General Jaruzelski was persuaded by strikes in many Polish factories during the summer to negotiate with Solidarity, and after a few months of preparation the Polish Round Table debate started in February 1989. The Berlin Wall started to shake.

Waldemar Fydrych, disgusted with the bad taste of political struggle in democratic Poland and not willing to be a public *persona*, left the country. Since 1990 he has lived in Paris.

Laughter as a Means of Struggle

Today, nine years after the decline of Orange Alternative's activities, we can see it as a movement proclaiming a radical political breakthrough. Every totalitarian order has its many inviolate rules. One of these is that the only means of conveying official political messages is the political force which dominates public life. The smallest independent message expressed in such a society poses a threat to the coherence and unity of public life and, in consequence, to the nature and existence of totalitarian power itself. If this takes on the form of a carnivalized celebration, with a predominance of joy, parody, and laughter, the end of the regime is clearly signalled.

In his sociological analysis of the events of May 1968 in Paris, Jean Duvignaud suggests that every revolution is a sudden 'discovery' of social groupings which have been discriminated against. Their representatives then seize the right to manifest and declare themselves, to present their new models of thinking and behaviour. The great feast of revolution enables 'the collective substance' to 'present itself' to its participants in acts of realizing hopes, emotions, and relations.

Such a 'self-presentation' of a 'discriminated class' (which, in our case, was almost the whole nation) had already taken place in Poland during the 'Solidarity carnival' of 1980–81. Then, the Orange Alternative was a child-like, criss-cross reference to the social 'performance' given by the whole of society during that period. There was nothing new to declare. After the ominous, bloody events of 1981–82 laughter, parody, and satire were the most efficient means of political struggle.

During the breakthrough of 1988–89 and in the following years there was, then, no revolution in Poland, because the revolutionary action had taken place eight years before. In 1989–90 there was only a very fast, sometimes very painful process of building up the basis of an open, free, democratic state and society which has been going on until today.

Of course the political analysis presented above does not cover all the aspects of activity in the Wrocław movement. Major declared himself an artist; he drew upon the traditions of surrealism; and the street events that he organized were called 'happenings'. From the first of his activities, he fought not only against Communist power but – perhaps first and foremost – against any stereotypical, narrow-minded understanding of the human condition in the late twentieth century, any way of life subordinated to the directives of science and philosophy. His surrealism was anarchistic in nature.

One common goal of contemporary philosophy, art, and literature has been to make man/woman a unity again. Such a goal has been declared many times in theory but very rarely has it been realized in artistic practice. Many high-sounding or mystifying phrases have been spoken or written without visible effect. The problem is that the truth about contemporary man/woman lies at a 'lower' level of human life – in the 'basis' rather than the 'superstructure', in the 'subconscious' rather than the 'conscious', in the 'existence' rather than the 'essence'.

Only works of art which enable us to find ourselves on this level and show us new existential perspectives are worthy of love and respect. Art cannot liberate us, cannot make us a unity again. It may, however, offer us an example of freedom – an intuitive glimpse of what that freedom would be like for us.[5]

Orange Alternative was a protest against a world subordinated to the utopian doctrine determined by a scientific paradigm of thought. We may, however, see in its actions an artistic assault upon public space. It was thus that Świdnicka Street, in the very centre of Wrocław – which before Major's *conquista* was grey and anonymous, ruled by routine, totally captive – began to ring with laughter, to become the first sign of the liberation of 'real existence' in Poland. The political liberation came later.

In spite of the ephemeral success of Orange Alternative, we are still waiting for a true surrealistic and anarchistic revolution. Major lives in Paris now, and maybe – as Lenin did in Zürich – he is trying to rethink his revolutionary strategy. And then, maybe, one day . . . .

Notes and References

1. Waldemar Fydrych, Bogdan Dobosz, 'Hokuspokus, czyli Pomaranczowa Alternatywa' ('Hocus-pocus or Orange Alternative'). Wrocław: *Inicjatywa Wydawnicza Aspekt, Wydawnictwo Kret*, April 1989, p. 8. All other quotations indicated by page numbers only are from this source.

2. Wojejech Marchlewski, 'Kronika zdarzen' ('The Chronicle of Events'), in 'Pomarariczowa Alternatywa, *Wigilia Wielkiej Rewolucji Pazdziernikowej*: próby zapisu ('Orange Alternative, *The Eve of the Great October Revolution*: an Attempt at Description', *Dialog*, No. 395 (August 1989), p. 119-24.

3. Marian Kozłowski, 'Czy istnieje taka alternatywa?' ('Does Such an Alternative Exist?'), *Gazeta Robotnicza*, No. 12,037 (1988), *Weekly Magazine*, No. 1,375 (4 March 1988), p. 7.

4. 'Wiosna, panie majorze! Rozmowa z rzecznikiem prasowym Ministra Spraw Wewnetrznych, mjr Wojciechem Garstka Rozmawia Julian Bartosz' ('It is Spring, Mr. Major! An interview by Julian Bartosz with the Spokesman of the Minister of Internal Affairs, Major Wojciech Garstka'), *Sprawy i Ludzie*, No. 311 (24 March 1988) p. 2.

5. This analysis is based on an essay written in 1963 by Konstanty Jelenski, published as 'O kilku sprzecznosciach sztuki wspolczesnej' ('On Several Contradictions of Contemporary Art'), in *Res Publica*, No. 3 (1987). Jelenski (1922–1987) was a Polish emigrant, essayist, and collaborator in the Paris monthly *Kultura*.

Aleks Sierz

Cool Britannia? 'In-Yer-Face' Writing in the British Theatre Today

The appearance of a succession of controversial and attention-catching new plays on the British stage in the 'nineties has led to considerable public discussion – and not a little ostensible outrage. In 'an interim report', Aleks Sierz examines the rash of plays about sex, drugs, and violence – notably *Trainspotting*, *Blasted*, *Mojo*, and *Shopping and Fucking* – by twenty-something authors, and asks whether they have anything in common beyond a flamboyant theatricality and the desire to shock. After showing how Cool Britannia's manifestation on the national stage has provoked arguments for and against this 'in-yer-face' drama, he outlines some of the common themes – such as the crisis of masculinity and the postmodern sensibility – that characterize much contemporary new writing. He argues that while these young writers are certainly gifted and mature, only subsequent theatrical revivals of their work will show whether it has anything lasting to say. Aleks Sierz is theatre critic for *Tribune*, and currently writing a book about 'in-yer-face' drama.

THE FIRST TIME I saw Mark Ravenhill's *Shopping and Fucking*, in October 1996, I sat just behind a black down-and-out making the most of the Royal Court's 10p standing tickets to shelter from the cold night. During the play, the tramp's bemused glances at the mainly white, middle-class audience were eloquent: what were these nice people doing watching these horrors? And, just to prove that new writing can keep a new audience, he came back after the interval.

This homeless vagrant was not the only person both puzzled and appalled by what happened on stage. Seasoned critics and audiences continue to debate the significance of the new wave of young writing in British theatre in the 'nineties. It is time to take stock of the claims made by the advocates of this new writing and to delineate its main characteristics.

The sudden appearance of 'in-yer-face', rude and crude, sexually explicit, and often violent plays by young and (usually) male writers is not an isolated phenomenon, but an aspect of the putative cultural renaissance much hyped as Cool Britannia. In 1996, the media – led by *Newsweek*, *Time*, *Le Monde*, and London's *Evening Standard* – repackaged London as the 'capital of cool'. By April 1998,

even Prime Minister Tony Blair was taking Cool Britannia seriously.[1] But while Cool Britannia was principally about cultural industries such as Brit pop and Brit film, traditional art forms such as theatre were soon gathered into the movement. Whether on the superficial level of marketing, or on the broader level of a creative upsurge, theatre was suddenly newsworthy again. Wherever you looked, there seemed to be young playwrights eager to cut their teeth on the zeitgeist.

Plays such as Sarah Kane's *Blasted*, Jez Butterworth's *Mojo*, and Mark Ravenhill's *Shopping and Fucking* were not only reviewed on the arts pages, they also became news. Hype like this either heralds events or follows them. In the case of theatre, the hype followed a rash of funky new plays by young authors. While the Royal Court marketed *East Is East*, a debut by Ayub Khan-Din, as 'seen by more people than any play in our history', Sarah Hemming wrote: 'The wave of young writing that has poured out of the theatre during [Stephen] Daldry's leadership has brought a fizz and excitement to new drama, reasserting its relevance.'[2]

If sceptics doubted whether there was anything really new about these plays, what certainly did change was the rhetoric surrounding new writing: while in the early 'nineties, critics were concerned about its demise, by the middle of the decade they were celebrating a new burst of creativity.

From Crisis to Creativity

For example, in May 1991 the critic of The Guardian, Michael Billington, described 'new writing' as 'in a state of crisis', pointing out that 'new drama no longer occupies the central position it has in British theatre over the past 35 years'.[3] By 1996, however, the discourse was much more upbeat. Billington, who has been the regular Guardian critic since 1971, wrote: 'I cannot recall a time when there were so many exciting dramatists in the twenty-something age-group: what is more, they are speaking to audiences of their own generation.'

Over in The Times, Benedict Nightingale pointed out how John Osborne's Look Back in Anger 'caused such a stir that the theatre was clearly "the place to be at",' and sensed that 'there is a similar buzz in the air now'. A year later, Nightingale characterized the new wave as 'a Theatre of Urban Ennui, marked by its abrasive portraits of city life'.[4] Plays nominated for this category usually include Nick Grosso's Peaches, Judy Upton's Bruises, Rebecca Prichard's Essex Girls, Joe Penhall's Some Voices, and Simon Bent's Goldhawk Road.[5]

Not many academics were as sensitive as the critics to changes in the cultural climate. It may be that, since direct arts funding by the British state was effectively cut in the early 'nineties, no one expected an outburst of creativity. In 1994, while Theodore Shank could write that 'It is fortunate that there is a continuous stream of young artists that do not carry the baggage of the past, artists who can look anew at our world', he could also say that theatre 'is lethargic and clumsy in its response to the changing emotive climate of a culture'.[6]

Nor were theatre practitioners fully aware of what was happening. When, in November 1994, the artistic directors of theatres all over Britain were asked by 87 playwrights to put on a quota of three new plays a year, the initiative was already outdated – elsewhere, other creative spirits were taking the changing cultural temperature of the times, and barely two months later the media attention that greeted Sarah Kane's debut, Blasted, at the Royal Court, seemed to signal the arrival of a new era.

The notoriety that Blasted immediately achieved suggests that historians may be tempted to date the start of theatre's Cool Britannic phase from the play's premiere on 12 January 1995. They would be wrong to do so. Other plays had used similar shock tactics. One year earlier, Anthony Neilson's Penetrator at the same venue was so 'in-yer-face' that critic Ian Herbert called for 'self-censorship'. Then, three months later, Philip Ridley's Ghost from a Perfect Place prompted Michael Billington to debate the play's 'quasi-pornographic' feel with its director, Matthew Lloyd, and the Hampstead Theatre's artistic director Jenny Topper. Lloyd defended the play's 'engagement with the present', while Topper said it was 'bold, innovative and exciting'.[7] Just as Hollywood was rediscovering the pulling power of such controversially violent films as Pulp Fiction or Natural Born Killers, British theatre was taking up violence as a way of exploring social issues.

Although the Royal Court Theatre has been central to the promotion of controversial new young writers, not everyone agrees that the phenomenon started there. Dominic Dromgoole, former artistic director of the Bush Theatre in west London, argues that the first preview of Jonathan Harvey's Beautiful Thing at that venue – in July 1993, eighteen months before Blasted – was 'one of the more significant nights in post-war theatre'. After this, new writing 'would never be the same again. . . . Beautiful Thing was the tip of the battering ram which knocked down the wall of dogma and defeatism' in British theatre.[8] The fact that there are different contenders for the title of first play of the current new wave shows that Cool Britannia has always been contested territory. Although it is not 'in-yer-face', Beautiful Thing is a good contender for one reason – its theme is the crisis of masculinity.

The debate about new plays by bright young wordsmiths has been played out in conferences, panels of commentators, on broadcast arts programmes, and in print. One of the prime advocates of new writing has been David Edgar. His postgraduate course in playwriting studies at Birmingham University taught many of the new wave: of the 90 graduates of the MA, which started in 1989, about one-third have become professional playwrights, including Sarah Kane, Clare Bayley, Ben Brown, and Rod Dungate.

The course's eighth annual conference, in April 1997, was called 'About Now' and discussed the new wave. 'Clearly', as Edgar said, 'over the past three or four years, there has been an immense growth in exciting new writing by people under thirty.'

Five years ago, sure, theatre was on life support. Suddenly, now, we're told, the stage has gone spicy. First nights are hip again. There are brat-packs, rude-broods and post-Tarantinians. There's even loose talk about a new golden age.[9]

Blokedom in Crisis

While in the 'eighties it was plays by women that spearheaded new writing, Edgar argued that now it was the turn of 'the *Boys' Own* play'. 'We are seeing a revival of the all-male play', he said, citing West End hits such as Tim Firth's *Neville's Island* (1994) and Patrick Marber's *Dealer's Choice* (1995) as boys' bonding plays, or gay plays such as Jonathan Harvey's *Beautiful Thing* (1993) and Kevin Elyot's *My Night with Reg* (1994), plus lads' plays such as Nick Grosso's *Peaches* and Simon Bent's *Goldhawk Road*. Just when commentators were confining laddism to television and the tabloids, it booted its way centre stage.

For masculinity and its discontents, Edgar argued, 'is *the* big subject of the 'nineties; just look at Yasmina Reza's *Art*'. If the most successful contemporary plays are often about blokes, they usually see blokedom as problematic. One variant of the boys' play is the 'girl-in-a-boys'-gang play'. Harry Gibson's version of *Trainspotting* and Ravenhill's *Shopping and Fucking* are good examples. In the latter, one woman holds a male milieu

together, and the news from the frontline of the sex war is not very good: when the boys find themselves up against the wall, they need a woman to help out. If they don't get one, they're in real trouble.

The new 'in-yer-face' plays owe much to American models. As Edgar said:

Okay, we'd lost the knack of hitting the zeitgeist where it hurt. But it was cruel indeed to find that as we dropped the baton, the Yanks had picked it up. . . . The two texts that really turned things around were *Angels in America* and *Oleanna* in 1993 – they reminded British theatre of the sort of play we used to do so well. A lot of people sensed that if American writers could write seriously and imaginatively about today's issues, then so could younger British writers.

The Royal Court under Stephen Daldry helped new writers and the National Theatre under Richard Eyre also set an example:

New work by old hands such as David Hare and Alan Bennett proved to young writers that the obituaries of new writing were very much exaggerated – they demonstrated that here was something that really could be thrilling and central.

But what about politics? 'When there's a core of writers for whom politics is not in the foreground, this raises the question of what political theatre is any more', Edgar said. 'After all, although *Trainspotting*, *Blasted*, or *Shopping and Fucking* may not be state-of-the-nation plays, they certainly do analyze a social milieu that's in crisis, and that's a political statement.' While the 'big political play' was no longer being written by people under the age of thirty, the reasons for this might be geo-political: 'After the collapse of Communism, it's surely no surprise that alternatives to our present set-up are hard to find. And so political drama is no longer centre stage.'

But the new writers were certainly gifted. 'What's striking is how mature the younger writers – such as Martin McDonagh, Rebecca Prichard, or David Eldridge – are in terms of their craft,' Edgar argued. 'Their writing has both vitality and good craftsmanship.' If 'a lot of new writing is conservative in form, this doesn't apply to the content. And although most new work is naturalistic,

'Something's missing. I need a tie or something.' David Westhead as Mickey and Tom Hollander as Baby in Jez Butterworth's *Mojo*, Royal Court main stage, London, July 1995. 'Fifties Soho gets the 'nineties design makeover. Photo: Ivan Kyncl.

accessible, and domestic, there are also exceptions, such as Martin Crimp's postmodernist *Attempts on Her Life.'*

Edgar did warn against complacency. 'The bad side of the current boom in new work is the element of fashion – this leads some people to think that last year the in-thing was smack, and this year it's sodomy. This can lead to dangerous mannerism.' Not so much a case of trainspotting as trend-spotting.

Not a Golden Age?

It was against this element of hype that critics of the new wave have reacted most sharply. One of the first was Peter Ansorge, author of a classic account of fringe theatre, *Disrupting the Spectacle* (1974), and until 1998 head of drama commissioning at Channel Four. At the 'About Now' conference – and in a subsequent book, *From Liverpool to Los Angeles* – he criticized the idea of a new wave. Ansorge's argument was that today's

theatre is not experiencing a golden age because most new work is superficial in its writing, ghettoized in its presentation, and lacking in the kind of writer/director partnerships which gave continuity to previous new waves.

While in the past writers such as John Osborne or Arnold Wesker addressed a wide mainstream culture, contemporary new plays flatter their audiences rather than engaging with them, confirm prejudices rather than questioning them, and talk to their own 'tribes' rather than to a general constituency: 'Even seemingly controversial work, like *Mojo* or *Trainspotting*, appeals to a targeted audience who share the writers' and directors' relish for Tarantino and drug culture.'[10]

Ansorge showed how the growth of small studio theatres tended to encourage writers to preach to the converted. And, finally, he attacked the postmodern mannerism of the most popular revival of the decade, Daldry's version of *An Inspector Calls*, comparing its spectacular ending – when a mansion

Toilet seat, not kitchen sink: Ewen Bremner as Mark in Harry Gibson's version of Irvine Welsh's *Trainspotting*, Bush Theatre, London, March 1995. The streetwise clothes contrast with the squalor of the squat. Photo: Mark Douet.

Hare, these new writers – at least according to Nightingale – have almost nothing to say.'[11]

Edgar and Ansorge are highly individual critics, but their views have been echoed in numerous media reports. For example, the director Matthew Warchus called 'plays about drugs and violence' 'reactionary and really uninteresting', while Ian Herbert compared the concern of Hare's generation with 'mass violence' to that of today's young writers with 'more personal acts of violence, such as rape or abuse'.[12]

On the one side, then, the advocates of Cool Britannia see new writing as part of a search for a modern national identity, and point out that new writers, if not constituting a new movement, are tackling important issues. On the other side, the sceptics emphasize the differences in quality between the 'nineties and earlier new waves. Who is right?

Four 'Dirty' Plays

In terms both of popularity and of controversy, the four most significant examples of Cool Britannia in the contemporary British theatre are *Trainspotting*, *Blasted*, *Mojo*, and *Shopping and Fucking*.[13] These plays clearly have characteristics in common: exuberant in language, they are also wildly, sometimes wonderfully foul-mouthed.

A much-quoted example comes from *Mojo*: 'When Silver Johnny sings the song my pussy hair stands up' (p. 4). Butterworth's language is splendidly elaborate and colourful. His technique is to set up a situation in plain language – 'they shit when he sings' – before repeating the sentiment in a more baroque style: 'polite young ladies come their cocoa in public' (p. 5).

If 'cunt' is still a taboo word, all of these plays break this taboo: Kane makes Ian, her main male character, say it eleven times while masturbating (p. 56). And throughout *Blasted* Kane shows male and female psychology through simple, flinty, and laconic dialogue which has been compared to that of Edward Bond. Often semi-articulate, it is also powerful and concise – as in Ian's:

collapses on stage – with Andrew Lloyd Webber's falling chandelier in *The Phantom of the Opera*.

Ansorge was quick to point out that the problem with the likes of Billington and Nightingale is that they suggest that new writing 'should command our interest without saying why'. Charting the way in which writers' visions have 'become small-scale', he claimed that new plays 'do not seem to suggest the kind of metaphor that might get an audience talking about their content and meaning' – and so they remain ghettoized. 'Unlike Osborne, Pinter, Shaffer, Brenton, or

'I've shat in better places than this': Pip Donaghy as Ian and Kate Ashfield as Cate in Sarah Kane's *Blasted*, Royal Court Theatre Upstairs, London, January 1995. Stage directions specify 'a very expensive hotel room in Leeds – the kind that is so expensive it could be anywhere'. Photo: Ivan Kyncl.

Can't always be taking it backing down letting them think they've got a right turn the other cheek SHIT some things are worth more than that have to be protected from shite.

Another is the Soldier's 'Saw thousands of people packing into trucks like pigs trying to leave town' (p. 31, 47). Kane's use of the present continuous tense is characteristic.

Like the Irvine Welsh novel on which it is based, *Trainspotting* is both humorous and sinister, its Leith demotic inescapably funny and lurid. Whether borrowing from rhyming slang ('Ah'm happy steying oan the rock 'n' roll [dole]', p. 18), or playfully vulgar ('You'd shag the crack ay dawn if it had hairs oan it!', p. 44), or cruelly revealing of its characters' hopelessness (junkie Alison prefers heroin to sex, saying 'That [drug injection] beats any meat injection', p. 26), *Trainspotting* is loaded with metaphors as addictive as its subject-matter.

Similarly, the jokes in Mark Ravenhill's work reveal a love of playful language on almost every page. In one striking image, a penis is a 'veiny bang stick' (p. 71). A description of 'lick and go' sex neatly sums up the play's themes of alienation and consumerism: 'We did a deal. I paid him. We confined ourselves to the lavatory. It didn't mean anything' (p. 17).

Elsewhere, Ravenhill's knowing and self-conscious 'way with words' can be sampled through his hectic use of parody. His favourites are contemporary discourses such as therapy-speak ('I have this personality you see? Part of me that gets addicted. I have a tendency to define myself purely in terms of my relationship to others', p. 30), or Ecstasy drug-talk ('I felt. I was looking down on this planet. Spaceman over this earth', p. 37), or postcolonial discourse ('You've got all the tastes in the world. You've got an empire under cellophane. Look, China. India. Indonesia. In the past you'd have to invade', p. 59).

Shared Imagery and Themes

In terms of stage imagery, drugs, sex, and violence dominate these plays. In *Trainspotting*, a female junkie's baby dies and a male injects himself in the penis. In *Blasted* there are scenes of rape (male and female), masturbation, defecation, blinding, and cannibalism – not gratuitous so much as unrelenting. In *Mojo*, a pair of dustbins are brought on stage – they hold the severed halves of the father of one of the characters; one young man is strung up by the ankles, another is shot in the head. Most of the men are high on amphetamines, which partly explains their verbal motormouthing.

In *Shopping and Fucking*, there is nudity, anal kissing – with the stage direction '*pulls away. There's blood around his mouth*' (p. 24) – and male rape, albeit consensual. Yet the undoubted strength of these plays lies not just in their linguistic virtuosity nor yet in their powerful stage images, but, as their advocates point out, in their undeniable theatricality.

Trainspotting has four actors (three male, one female) doubling parts. With its direct address to the audience, narrative speeches, and imaginative use of simple props, it demonstrates the power of rough theatre. Unlike the sanitized film version, it doesn't have a heist plot, but two scenes of 'in-yer-face' feminism instead. In *Mojo*, which is about petty villains, the Beckettian dustbins are joined by other visual gags – involving objects such as toffee apples, cake-boxes, or a tiny gun – which comically counterpoint the violence. All are vividly theatrical.

In *Blasted*, the ending – in which rains falls on a man's eyeless head poking out of the floorboards while a young woman, blood running down her legs, shares her food with him – is an unforgettable picture of humanity amid horror which refers as much to Bosnia as to Beckett. In *Shopping and Fucking*, the scene where an 'actress' auditions topless while reciting Chekhov is not only an apt image of the search for work, but also a theatrical in-joke. The play's other themes are aptly expressed in symbols such as the television dinners, the bag of coins won in an arcade slot-machine, and the videos of sex, a boy playing a violin, and a man being tortured.

All four 'dirty' plays also share strong thematic concerns. They are all boys' plays.

'Take your jacket off.' Robin Soans as Brian and Kate Ashfield as Lulu in Mark Ravenhill's *Shopping and Fucking*, Royal Court Theatre Upstairs, London, October 1996. Flashing neon signs signal the play's critique of voyeurism. Photo: John Haynes.

In *Blasted*, war is seen as an excretion of masculine psychology; in *Trainspotting*, the boys make up a gang which has dubious attitudes to women; in *Mojo*, there are no female characters – the men behave as if still in a playground; in *Shopping and Fucking*, the boys are confused by gender roles and it is the Lulu character who holds their male milieu together.

As Ian Rickson, Daldry's successor at the Royal Court, said: 'One of the most important issues of the late twentieth century has been the crisis in masculinity – in the workplace and the family – and that's why there's been a lot of boys' plays.'[14] Yet, although all four plays explore the theme of masculinity as somehow in crisis, none offers an alternative vision of what it could be to be a man at the end of the twentieth century. And while each of the plays by male authors is hip enough to wink at feminism, each also exploits elements of 'lad culture'.

All four plays sparked controversy. *Trainspotting* was attacked for glamorizing drugs; *Blasted* was denounced by the *Daily Mail* as 'this disgusting feast of filth'; *Mojo* was criticized for its dehumanization of violence and *Shopping and Fucking* for its title, its sex scenes, and its bad taste. Perhaps the severest criticism is that these plays, like much other new writing, have 'no heart'. They lack compassion and humanism.

Unlike the great liberal dramas of past new waves, the politics of the plays are implicit rather than explicit. For example, Ravenhill has argued that his play is an implicit critique of Thatcher's dictum that 'There is no such thing as society' – it captures the 'low-level anger of the twenty-to-thirty generation' – while Daldry claims that young audiences no longer want the old-fashioned thesis play, but prefer 'a personalized internal search with not necessarily a clear answer'.[15] Perhaps the plays' critiques of modern society are muffled by their subjectivity – and by their attraction to a distinctly postmodern sensibility.

Surfing on Postmodernity

Often concerned with surface rather than with depth, these plays *are* all postmodern – but in different ways. At times, they seem to exemplify Ansorge's idea that 'when new writers do turn to narrative, the main influences often come from film and television'. With its parodies of discourse, *Shopping and Fucking* is perhaps most conscious of the intellectual zeitgeist. At one point, Robbie says:

A long time ago there were big stories. Stories so big you could live your whole life in them. The powerful Hands of the Gods and Fate. The Journey to Enlightenment. The March of Socialism. But they all died or the world grew up or grew senile and forgot them, so now we're all making up our own stories (p. 63).

Robbie – or Ravenhill – has obviously been reading Jean-François Lyotard's theory of the end of grand narratives.[16] In other scenes, the mixture of high and low culture – most ridiculously during the episode when Lulu sells sex by phone, encouraging a punter with a mix of Renaissance literary language and crude slang (p. 50) – also marks out the play as postmodern.

In its savage fracture between a naturalistic first half and a nightmarish second, *Blasted* has a postmodernist structural form. Kane sees this as the key to its scandalized reception: 'Because *Blasted* didn't have a conventional story-line and there was no precedent in terms of its structure, people didn't have a context in which to locate it.'[17] Thematically, its idea that there is a congruence between populist media discourses and the act of war also evokes a contemporary sensibility.

In *Mojo*, the mixing of genres – combining Pinteresque verbal menace with Tarantino-style physical violence – is its most evident sign of postmodernism. Not only does the play's highly charged surface glitter take priority over plot, character, or depth, but there is a fracture of historical eras: although set in 'fifties Soho, the play's language is 'nineties Hollywood. This mixture extends to the way it turns its vicious last scene into comedy. As one critic said: 'The audience is helpless with laughter. We have been dehumanized, and we're loving it.'[18]

In *Trainspotting* there is much less evidence of a postmodern sensibility, despite the piece's debt to William Burroughs's *The Naked Lunch* and other classics of drug culture. Rather, it is postmodern in its relationship to other media – first a cult book by Irvine Welsh, then a play, and finally a film, *Trainspotting* exemplifies the way a cultural icon can cross the media divide. The play version is less an *adaptation* of the book than a *staging* of some of its many narratives.

The Survival Factor

With their emphasis on sex, drugs, and violence, the 'in-yer-face' debuts by twenty-something authors are a distinct theatrical phenomenon. Although part of a general hype about Cool Britannia, plays such as

Trainspotting, Blasted, Mojo, and *Shopping and Fucking* have not been assimilated easily into mainstream culture. Touring productions – and film versions – of the plays have excited fresh controversy. Not only do they articulate a specifically 'nineties zeitgeist – with their (often implicit) critique of contemporary gender roles and consumerist society – but they have also been instrumental in the remaking of Britain's national image.

Sceptics who claim that such plays are not much good often compare them unfavourably with the products of previous new waves. Of course, 'in-yer-face' drama is not strong on either plot or characterization – but its power lies in the directness of its shock tactics, the immediacy of its language, the relevance of its themes, and the stark aptness of its stage pictures.

In a decade when Arts Council funding has been at a standstill, it is worth acknowledging that the unexpected eruption of a score of fresh young writers represents a triumph of creativity over scarce resources. If many new writers no longer enjoy long-term relationships with a patron institution, but have to commute between writing for stage and for screen, their job insecurity mirrors that of the rest of the workforce in a post-Thatcher era. Because it is unlikely that writers of such calibre will be content to repeat the shock tactics that made their early work controversial, the future of the new drama lies in increasing individual diversity. In this sense, 'in-yer-face' theatre is perhaps a temporary phenomenon rather than a movement.

The final judgement on theatre's Cool Britannia will not be literary or political or cultural, but theatrical. Revivals of modern classics prove their theatrical vitality, even when the circumstances that informed their writing have changed. Plays such as *Trainspotting, Blasted, Mojo,* and *Shopping and Fucking* owe much to their original directors and casts. Future revivals will show whether the issues they addressed so urgently have outlived their sell-by date – or whether they've become an established part of the theatrical vocabulary of social criticism.

Notes and References

1. See the cover article, 'Why London Rules', *Newsweek,* 4 November 1996; *Sunday Times,* 5 April 1998.

2. Jess Cleverly, fund-raising letter, Royal Court, December 1997; Sarah Hemming, *The Independent,* 18 February 1998, p. 14.

3. Michael Billington, *One Night Stands: a Critic's View of Modern British Theatre* (London: Nick Hern, 1993), p. 360.

4. *The Guardian,* 13 March 1996; *The Times,* 1 May 1996; *The Times,* 14 May 1997. See also Benedict Nightingale, *The Future of Theatre* (London: Phoenix, 1998), p. 17–22.

5. See anthologies such as *Coming on Strong: New Writing from the Royal Court Theatre,* including *Peaches* and *Essex Girls* (London: Faber, 1995), and *Bush Theatre Plays* (London: Faber, 1996). It is, however, significant that the Bush anthology features plays by women, most of which fall neither into the 'urban ennui' nor 'lads' play' categories.

6. Theodore Shank, ed., *Contemporary British Theatre* (London: Macmillan, 1994), p. 18.

7. Ian Herbert, 'Prompt Corner', *Theatre Record,* XIV, No. 1 (January 1994), p. 3; *The Guardian,* 23 April 1994.

8. See Michael Thornton, 'A Shop Window for Outrage', *Punch,* 21–27 September 1996; Dromgoole, in Mike Bradwell, ed., *The Bush Theatre Book* (London: Methuen, 1997), p. 70–5.

9. Personal interview with Aleks Sierz, March 1997; Aleks Sierz, 'The Write Stuff', *The Independent,* 9 April 1997; Michael Coveney, 'Play Fighting', *The Observer,* 20 April 1997; David Edgar, 'Eighth Birmingham Theatre Conference Paper', in *Studies in Theatre Production,* No. 15 (June 1997), p. 80–1; Aleks Sierz, ' "About Now" in Birmingham', *New Theatre Quarterly,* No. 51 (August 1997), p. 289–90; David Edgar, 'Plays for Today', *Sunday Times,* 7 September 1997.

10. Peter Ansorge, *From Liverpool to Los Angeles* (London: Faber, 1997), p. 11, 140, 118–19.

11. Ibid.

12. Warchus, quoted in *Time Out,* 15–22 April 1998, p. 137; Ian Herbert, 'Prompt Corner', *Theatre Record,* XVIII, No. 6 (March 1994), p. 317.

13. Published as Irvine Welsh, *Trainspotting* and *Headstate* (London: Minerva, 1996); Sarah Kane, *Blasted and Phaedra's Love* (London: Methuen, 1996); Jez Butterworth, *Mojo* (London; Nick Hern, second ed., 1996); Mark Ravenhill, *Shopping and Fucking* (London: Methuen, second ed., 1997).

14. *Theatreland,* London Weekend Television, 8–9 March 1998. Books such as Nick Hornby's *Fever Pitch* and *High Fidelity,* or films such as *Brassed Off* and *The Full Monty,* indicate that the theme of masculinity in crisis is central to the wider culture.

15. See James Macdonald in *Royal Court Newsletter* (March–June 1998), p. 2; Carl Miller, 'Shocking and Fussing', http://www.royal-court.org.uk (July 1997); 'Do New Writers Have Hearts?' *New Sceptics,* Session 1, Theatre Museum, 15 October 1996.

16. Ansorge, op cit., p. 60–1. See Jean-François Lyotard, *The Postmodern Condition: a Report on Knowledge* (Manchester University Press, 1984).

17. Kane, quoted in *Time Out,* 25 March–1 April 1998, p. 27.

18. Ian Herbert, 'Prompt Corner', *Theatre Record,* XV, No. 15 (July 1995), p. 945.

Catherine Diamond

Darkening Clouds over Istanbul: Turkish Theatre in a Changing Climate

Modern Turkish theatre, benefiting from the support of the founder of the Turkish Republic, Mustapha Kemal Ataturk, has had a secular bent throughout its history. However, after the elections of 1994 and 1995, when Refah (Welfare) Party candidates espousing a distinctly religious agenda swept into power, dramatists have found themselves in an uneasy position, caught between corrupt secular politicians and a censorship-inclined military on the one hand, and Islamists hostile to theatre both in principle and as an unnecessary luxury on the other. Besides swiftly changing demographics and competition from alternative entertainments, shifts in political policy in Istanbul are eroding the city's strong theatre tradition. Yet the theatre of this nation which straddles Europe and Asia maintains an impressive vitality and variety, with state and municipal companies mounting regular seasons of foreign and Turkish works, and experimental troupes challenging established theatre forms as well as daring to broach some of the sensitive ideological conflicts in Istanbul. Catherine Diamond, a dancer and drama professor in Taiwan, is author of *Sringara Tales*, a collection of short stories about dancers in South-East Asia and the Middle East.

THE ARMED STRUGGLE against the Kurdish quest for an independent homeland and the rise of an Islamic presence on its political front are two of the thorniest issues in Turkey's domestic affairs.[1] Since the Gulf War in 1991, which gave new impetus to the Kurdish independence movement, and the 1994 municipal and 1995 national elections, in which Islamic candidates won not only the mayoralties of all major Turkish cities, but also the appointment of Prime Minister, Turkish writers and dramatists have been caught in a conservative backlash. Freedom of expression has been curtailed both by religious groups and an increasingly draconian secularist government which is closely allied with the military.[2]

The situation, however, is only the latest configuration of Turkey's conflict, continuing through the twentieth century, between those pursuing Mustapha Kemal Ataturk's vision of a modern secular state that looked toward Europe, and those striving to preserve the legacy of the Ottoman empire, when the caliph in Istanbul was the religious leader of the Moslem Middle East.[3] In addition, the disintegration of the Soviet Union,

Turkey's large and powerful neighbour, has created a new sense of instability. The western countries of the NATO alliance, which were willing formerly to turn a blind eye to Turkey's internal problems in order to have an ally on the Soviet border, are now less comfortable overlooking blatant human rights violations. Theatre people working in Istanbul have weathered many political storms, but after the 1994–95 elections, they felt a new sense of urgency about the problems facing their art and their city.[4]

On 7 March 1996, one of Turkey's best-known novelists and playwrights, Yasar Kemal, was convicted of 'inciting hatred' and encouraging Kurdish separatism' in an essay, 'Dark Cloud over Turkey', that had appeared in *Der Spiegel*, and then in a book, *Freedom of Thought in Turkey*. Kemal accused the Turkish government of long having had a system of coercion and repression, concealed from its own people and from foreign governments. The campaign has been so fierce that it has left many wishing for a return to the pre-Republican autocracy, which, in turn, has fuelled the resurgence of Islamic political parties.[5]

Using harsh language, Kemal labelled the Turkish government's onslaught against the Kurdish people a genocidal massacre. The Kurds, most of whom would prefer peaceful co-existence inside Turkey to an independent homeland, are being treated as the vanguard of a nation-wide insurgency, which the secular government uses to justify more and increasingly drastic measures against all opposition.[6]

Kemal remained defiant throughout his trial, telling the court, 'I am being judged because I want the war to stop. I will fight until death for the end of this war. Jail me if you like. It is not you who sentence me. I condemn you.'[7] He was given a twenty-month suspended sentence under Article 8 of the new and severe Anti-Terrorism Act.

As columnist and newspaper publisher Ilnur Cevik astutely noted, it was not only Kemal's sentence but the conditions of its suspension that were ominous for others:

It seems the authorities could not afford jailing Kemal, so they decided to allow him to remain as a free man, provided he did not commit the same 'crime' again. . . . The very fact that Kemal was allowed to stay out of prison but was threatened to go to jail if he again spoke his mind is rather dangerous.[8]

Drawing attention from afar, Kemal received letters of support from the Swedish Writers' Union and playwright Arthur Miller; but, more importantly, Turkish writers and dramatists united behind Kemal, both to protest his case and to protect themselves.[9] No fewer than 1,089 writers collected their own articles and published them in a book, *Freedom of Expression and Turkey*. No sooner did the book come out than a few were arraigned on the same charges as Kemal, but what embarrassed the authorities is that many more showed up and demanded also to be charged. As of March 1996, 98 people have been charged.[10]

Among these was Mahir Gunsiray, an increasingly disenchanted actor with the State Theatre in Istanbul, who turned the court into a kafkaesque theatre of the absurd. When addressed by the judge, Gunsiray replied by quoting from Kafka's *The Trial*:

Why are you so silent now? Who are you? What are you doing here? Of course you are just obeying your orders. When you leave here, you'll go to your home and hug your wife and daughters. Do you have a conscience? Do you know what one is?[11]

A Sense of Creeping Fascism

Gunsiray, a graduate of Leeds University, has been something of a political gadfly on the Istanbul theatre scene, but, like many, he feels pressure from increased Islamic antipathy towards the theatre as well as from the military's intolerance of criticism. As a member of The Alternative Theatre (Oteki Tiyatro), in 1995 he performed in the play *Missing (Kaybolma)* which was later staged for both the Istanbul International Theatre Festival (in 1995) and the Bonn Biennial Theatre Festival (in June 1996). The play, created by the troupe, involves the cases of Turkish people who 'disappeared' in the events leading up to the military coup in 1980, and the kafkaesque bureaucracy facing their relatives when they tried to find out what had become of them – a controversial subject even in the 1990s.[12]

Concern with the creeping acceptance of evil and crimes against humanity in everyday life was the focus of another of Gunsiray's recent productions, Brecht's *A Man's a Man (Adam Adamdir*, 1996) which he co-directed with Cetin Sarikartal. Collaborating with a new experimental company, Tiyatro Ti,[13] mainly comprising recent graduates of the State Conservatory at Mimar Sinan University, Gunsiray explored the process by which fascism steals into the fabric of society. Its attack on civil liberties, he feels, is no longer cloaked in the full military regalia of the mid-twentieth century – of which people have learned to be wary – but permeates society and undermines it in a much more subtle fashion through media manipulation.

Combined with Brecht's foyer play, *The Elephant Calf* (which Gunsiray placed on stage with two clowns holding clappers to represent the audience), *A Man's a Man* depicts the odyssey of Galy Gay, a Chaplin-like character coerced into the British army in the India of the 1920s, and is a twentieth-century parable of turning man into machine. Beguiled into impersonating a missing soldier, Galy Gay first assumes a new name for convenience, although still maintaining his identity. But a mock execution forces him to complete the transition, and finally he embraces his false identity without any memory of the former.

His adaptability proves to be his undoing. Unaware of the process and the full extent of the powers working upon him, he differs from his 'classically' fascistic commander, whose identity is so enmeshed with power that, without it, he mutilates himself. Yet the inoffensive Galy Gay emerges as the more dangerous of the two.

Gunsiray clearly wanted the spectators to view the play in the light of current events. Without visually or otherwise adapting it to Turkey, he and the troupe implied the connection between the demise of individual identity and the rise of totalitarian power, especially that of religious fundamentalism. Contending that artists, being in the social vanguard and therefore more sensitive to such threats, have an obligation to warn people, Gunsiray feels that manipulation of the media and lack of diverse expression will be the most dangerous threat in the future.[14]

Gunsiray, who plays Bloody Five, the fascist commander who castrates himself, also suggests that Galy Gay mirrors the artists' condition of enduring demeaning conditions while maintaining a sense of an essential self. He is bothered by the 'flexibility' of some of his colleagues in the State Theatre who do not take individual responsibility and willingly cater to harmful interests rather than acknowledge the political consequences of their actions.[15]

Tiyatro Ti had staged only one previous production, a two-hander by Athol Fugard, *The Island*. Disillusioned with what they felt was the commercialism of the State Theatre and the lack of opportunity for young actors, members of Tiyatro Ti were trying to create good ensemble work. Private Turkish companies tend to work around a star, an actor-manager, and Tiyatro Ti wanted to perform professional quality work while preserving the *esprit de corps* of an ensemble.[16]

Gunsiray and Sarikartal used a rough and unpolished 'street theatre' style; however, the show's most original feature was a green room behind the stage. When not on stage, the characters waited in a green-lit box, maintaining their stage presence though not actively participating in the action. The green light gave them a sinister appearance as they formed tableaux not unlike that of Pirandello's *Six Characters in Search of an Author* when the six characters gather for their final mysterious pose – their identities caught in limbo, projecting their dilemma both as actors and as characters waiting, neither off stage nor on. Galy Gay's transition truly represented their assumption of their roles, the interplay of deceptive plasticity and artful truth.

For Gunsiray, unused to the western 'green room', green had an entirely different connotation in that it is the colour of Islam. 'I am surrounded by green', he said. And the glowing green off to one side was all that he needed to convey his anxiety.

The Political Fallout in Istanbul

Turkish theatre faced a new challenge from Islamist-led governments after the 1994–95 elections. Threatening to remove state support, members of the pro-Islamic Welfare Party (Refah) began closing theatres in some areas and promising further cuts. Speaking under the auspices of the Ministry of Culture, Zeki Unal, a Refah MP, said that those who patronized opera, ballet, and theatre should pay for the arts, not the state.[17]

The Municipal Theatre of Diyarbakir in eastern Turkey was closed with the argument that 'the municipality had no money to spare for theatre'. The cast was redeployed in other divisions of the city government.[18] Arts projects were subjected to more rigorous censorship and subtle dismantling.[19]

Perhaps nowhere were the performing arts placed in a more tenuous position than in Istanbul, where the pragmatic Islamist mayor set about aiding the urban poor.[20] No one in theatre was quite certain what the political fallout would be except that less money would be forthcoming. Small studios

336

Scenes from Tiyatro Ti's production of Brecht's *A Man's a Man*. Top: Taner Birsel as Galy Gay, buying the elephant calf. Bottom: Galy Gay undresses – note the observers behind the screen of the 'green room'.

formerly allotted to the various theatre groups for use as rehearsal spaces were claimed by Islamists, who converted them into *mescit*, or prayer halls.

One of the first people directly to feel the change was Gurun Gencay, the staunchly secular director of Istanbul's Municipal Theatre, who was removed from her position. Formerly a translator of western plays, primarily French, and a dramaturg in Ankara, Gencay favoured what she considered strong texts regardless of their origin. After her dismissal, she not only became a Member of Parliament but started her own company, Tiyatro Istanbul, which includes some of Turkey's most illustrious actors, such as Cihan Unal, while maintaining her personal penchant for strongly written scripts.

Gencay's ousting was a clear signal to uncompromising secularists, yet she herself was undaunted, quoting from her favourite play, Ionesco's *Rhinoceros*:

People who try to hang on to their individuality always come to a bad end. Oh, well, too bad. I'll take on all of them. I'll put up a fight against the lot of them, the whole lot of them. I'm the last man left, and I'm staying that way until the end. I'm not capitulating.[21]

In Beyoglu – a small separate municipality within Istanbul which is the entertainment district, and where most of the theatres are located – a campaign was launched against Nusret Bayraktan, the Refah candidate, because it was feared that a religious mayor would close down many of the establishments. When Bayraktan won none the less, he immediately tried to ban alchohol in the area, but this move met with resounding failure.

Many journalists have been circumspect about how they document the changes in the cultural life of the city. The *Turkish Daily News* reported:

Islamists have made inroads into the cultural salons which were previously forbidden to them, and Mayor Tayyip Erdogan has made the arts more accessible to a wider range of people. . . . While some artists and people of culture feel rather uncomfortable because of this Islamic

point of view, another group [unspecified] is happy because the gates have been opened for a dialogue. Moreover, the mayoralty and cultural policy of Refah, portrayed as revenge on the [artistic] community, has yet to result in something very bad. The Refah metropolitan mayoralty has followed a policy more inclusive of society in general than that carried out under the previous mayor, Nurettin Sozen, and has succeeded in opening the doors which had previously been shut to the Islamists. In the meetings which the municipality has been organizing, influence has been given to inviting those thinkers from Europe and the United States who look on a resurgent Islam with warmth and who are involved in propagating Islamic culture, yet there has still been little connection with Muslim Arab countries in the area of cultural exchange.[22]

The Problems of Islamic Interdiction

This cautious description implies a desire to turn away from western cultural influence and 'return' to more distinctly Turkish arts, although what those would be is not clear. Some surmised that the production of more Turkish plays in state and municipal theatres was intended, although these theatres already offer a balanced repertoire of foreign and locally written plays.

It would be very difficult to ascertain, moreover, what kind of theatrical exchange could take place with Turkey's Arab neighbours, since Turkey has the most developed theatre tradition and network in the Middle East.[23] Istanbul has held an international arts festival since 1973, and an independent theatre festival started in 1989 – but few Islamic countries have participated. In 1996, Diyarbakir played host to the 'Experimental Theatres Festival of Middle East Countries', but with the closing of the city's theatre and its cast dispersed into municipal offices the likelihood of similar exchanges in the near future must remain in doubt.

Fundamentalist interpretations of Islam have long had a reputation for being hostile to the representational performing arts, as Turkey's foremost theatre scholar, Metin And, summed up: 'Stage representation is against the Islamic doctrine, and the very essence of theatrical art demands representation which is repugnant and profane to Islamic theologians.'[24]

The Prophet Mohammed is said to have issued a ban on entertainment on the ground that it was a deviation from worship, leading to immoral behaviour and a transgression of God's will. In Turkey, however, performers found ways to circumvent the sanction in the three traditional performing arts: *karagoz*, the popular shadow puppetry that spread throughout the Middle East and the Balkans; *orta oyunu*, the uniquely Turkish drama that resembles *commedia dell'arte*; and the tradition of the *meddah*, or storyteller.

All have had to justify their function and suffer Mohammed's injunction against the representation of humans and animals, especially the human face, although *karagoz* received a special dispensation from the rule against representation: 'Many celebrated Sufi disciples used the image of the shadow theatre screen to illustrate their doctrine, and the shadow theatre itself, thanks to their mystical teaching, was widely accepted in Islamic countries, chiefly in Turkey.'[25]

The Moslem clergy, who, in general, came to enjoy *karagoz* performances, ingeniously circumvented the letter of the law:

The ban, they said, applies only to images of animate beings; and since the *karagoz* puppets are perforated with holes, they are no longer animate nor represent human flesh; consequently to attend the performances is permitted canonically. However, there remains the tradition of the Prophet by virtue of which the angel cannot penetrate into a house containing such images, and to keep puppets in an inhabited house is considered impious.[26]

No Turkish law actually forbade acting and plays, though there were specific interdictions against satiric representations of other religious groups, judges, priests, and teachers.

In Ottoman practice, *fetvas*, or sentences, given on a matter of Canon Law, delivered by Muftis, show the attitude towards theatrical spectacles: how the law prohibited only certain forms of imitation, acting as a censor to prevent any presentation which might belittle respected institutions like those of education, law, or religion.[27]

The clerics despised *orta oyunu*, but Metin And suggests that perhaps the actors had managed to develop a presentational and non-illusionistic theatre in order not to transgress the taboo on representation:

Orta oyunu, because of the nature of its means of expression and the quality of its rapport with the audience, can be called presentational or non-illusionistic. The actor does not lose his identity as an actor and shows his awareness of this to the audience. The audience does not regard him as pretending to be a real person but as an actor. The stage is not conceived as being discontinued and separated from the audience, there is no line between them, and no removed fourth wall. The actor keeps reminding the audience continuously that they sit in the theatre, and makes the audience part of the show. The actor therefore is permitted direct address to the audience.[28]

The storyteller, or *meddah* – which literally means 'panegyrist', or 'extoller' – had been a feature of Turkish life since before Turkey's conversion to Islam, and the epic literature of pre-Islamic Turkish groups was probably disseminated not only by the troubadours but also by the storytellers:

After conversion to Islam, the Turkish meddahs told their traditional tales of heroism, religious narratives of the new faith, and myths and legends taken over from the Persians, Indians, and Arabs. The *meddahs* not only provided live entertainment and a measure of intellectual stimulation but also served the function of propaganda, proselytizing unbelievers and reinforcing the faith of the believers. But the evangelical function as well as the Islamic content of the *meddahs*' stories were abandoned in time when the Mohammedan clergy forbade any reference to the saints in the plays.[29]

In the second half of the nineteenth century strict political censorship was also exercised on the *meddahs*, and all satire upon the sultan was forbidden.

The Work of Ferhan Sensoy

In Istanbul, the three forms are virtually defunct, but they have been absorbed into the modern Turkish theatre, and the strength of the *meddah* tradition might explain the unusual popularity of the monodrama in the present theatre. A contemporary dramatist who conscientiously incorporates the qualities of these traditional theatres is Ferhan Sensoy. A multi-talented satirist who writes, directs, and stars in his own plays, he has demonstrated a personal initiative that has stood him in good stead both financially and artistically, although he has been at loggerheads with political and religious conservatives in the past.

Sensoy, as director of his own company, Ortaoyuncular, has been both imprisoned and awarded for his work. Having studied at the Ecole Supériere d'Art Dramatique in Strasburg, he has been staging his own plays since 1973, a time when many private theatres were struggling to survive. He established Ortaoyuncular in 1980 – its name clearly affiliating it with *orta oyunu* – but in 1987, his *Obscene Musical* (*Muzir Muzikal*) was criticized by a conservative faction, and after its seventy-seventh performance the San Theatre, where it was showing, mysteriously burned down.

Sensoy himself was sentenced to a three-week prison term. Finding himself without a theatre and unsure of what to do next, he wrote a monodrama, *The World According to Ferhan* (*Ferhangi Seyler*), which, after one thousand performances and also a European tour, still remains one of his most popular shows.

Although few *meddahs* still exist, Sensoy represents a modern version and credits the famous masters as his teachers. He has converted the traditional into a contemporary idiom, and whether conscious of this technique or not, his audiences love his work, sometimes seeing a performance two or three times. His regularly sold-out performances demonstrate that this use of earlier popular forms offers an excellent resource without having to draw upon its old-fashioned content.[30]

Audiences keep coming back to see *The World According to Ferhan* because its improvisational format addresses the most current topics, and its required audience participation makes it a different show every night. Without another actor on stage, Sensoy calls upon members of the audience to fill in the necessary roles and adjusts his dialogue to their responses. He plays a writer, a single man alone in his apartment. He reads the newspaper and makes satirical comments on

topical issues, and in the first versions of the play that appeared right after the burning of the theatre, oblique references to conservatives peppered his caustic observations.

He calls up a female audience member to play the housekeeper and help him change the sheet on the bed, and then makes sexual advances to her, carefully modulating his performance to her reactions. He recalled one time when he was thoroughly upstaged by a woman who began taking off her clothes.[31]

The play begins with the actor arriving late on stage, and every night he tells a different story of why he has been delayed, thus playing with the transition between Ferhan the actor and Ferhan the character. Moreover, at one point, the lights go off, and somebody (a plant in the audience) asks if the theatre has a back-up generator. The audience and the character on stage all accept that the lights have gone off in the theatre, not Ferhan's apartment, thus the *orta oyunu* presentational style is maintained throughout.

'The Three Bullet Opera'

As with many other cultures that maintain traditional presentational forms of theatre, Turkey has had a penchant for Brecht.[32] Sensoy found *The Threepenny Opera*, Gay's *Beggar's Opera*, and *orta oyunu* wholly compatible, and adapted them into a *Three Bullet Opera*, a satire about current politics, the new Turkish mafia.

Old and new styles were easily mixed in this anachronistic production. Sensoy's Polly Peachum (played by his wife Derya Baykal Sensoy) was no modest lily but a seductive blonde who cajoles customers on the streets into buying her pretzels, a typical Turkish street snack. Although costumed like an eighteenth-century wench, she pulls her gum out before she kisses Binbela ('Cause Trouble') Mahmut, the Turkish Macheath whom Sensoy plays. Polly's mother is never without a glass of *raki*, the Turkish liquor, and Pirate Jenny, dressed in the silver lamé miniskirt of a contemporary prostitute, reads Turkish coffee-grounds while Mahmut calls

Scenes from Ferhan Sensoy's adaptation, *The Three Bullet Opera*, after Gay and Brecht. Top: Polly Peachum (Derya Baykal Sensoy) singing in her parents' rag shop. Bottom: Sensoy as Binbela Mahmut, accompanying himself on the *divan saz* in his prison cell. Photos: Hezarfen Fotografya.

his gang from a cellular phone and pays off the police with a personal cheque.

Before each song, the actors march up stage, whirl around, and come downstage singing, making a distinct break from the preceding scene – the convention not proving disruptive, but operating as a sign for a new orientation. The orchestra, consisting of piano, drums, and clarinet, played distinctively Turkish popular music. The set, designed by Sensoy, was minimal and versatile, consisting of a single back panel that rotated to one side to show a wall of old clothes being sold by old Peachum, and ... the bars of Mahmut's jail.

... he play begins, Peachum's beg-... through the theatre, accosting the ... , begging, and selling their wares.

... he Ses Theatre, the nineteenth-century ... peretta theatre Sensoy has refurbished, is on Istiklal Caddesi, in the heart of Beyoglu: still a pleasant street for a stroll, it is now filled with real beggars, young and old, many of whom are the displaced Kurds from Anatolia who have flocked to the city after their villages have been burned by guerrillas or government forces. Upon entering the theatre, one experiences an uncomfortable disjunction between the real and artificial demonstrations of poverty.

Sensoy modelled his Macheath more on Gay's version than Brecht's:

Gay's Mack the Knife was an outlaw admired by the common people. In Brecht's play, he is a pitiless burglar. Our character Binbela Mahmut is also an outlaw yet he admires Ataturk. Mahmut wears an Ataturk pin on his lapel. Actually we are not too far from Brecht, because in our play as well the deprived characters say the right things.[33]

In a long speech, Sensoy confirms the gangster's adulation of Ataturk, and by doing so expresses the attitude of many people who are not acquainted with the leader's specific precepts but still rally behind his legend as a defender of secular Turkey. Every night this speech meets with enthusiastic applause.

Sensoy, an urban satirist, has made Istanbul, rather than Turkey, his beat. *Three Bullet Opera* reveals his concern about the exploitation of the new urban poor in Istanbul, not only financially by mafia-like gangs, but politically by religious extremists as well.[34]

The Theatrical Tradition and the Poor

This shift in Istanbul's political climate is directly related to a drastic alteration in the city's demographics. In the 1960s – now considered the heyday of Turkish theatre – Istanbul's population stood at one million.[35] In 1996, it was 12 million and is expected to rise to some 23 million by the year 2000. The increase is caused by a massive inflow of peasants from other parts of Turkey, including large numbers of Kurds, who arrive poor, uneducated, and without skills to help them find work.

Although this swelling population casts its vote, and has been largely responsible for Refah's rise to power, it has neither interest in theatre nor money to attend. As Yildiz Kenter, Turkey's foremost actress, puts it: 'While the Istanbul population grows, the theatre audience dwindles.' Satellite television has displaced videos as the most popular form of entertainment, and dramatists fear that a citizenry enamoured of its generally poor-quality programming will never develop into one that can appreciate theatre and live performance. So, while the secular urban middle classes continue to patronize the theatre, the theatre itself is of scant concern to the ranks of the city's looming poor.

Although western theatre entered Istanbul and initially found favour in the Ottoman court in the mid nineteenth century, it was Ataturk's vision that was responsible for the impetus that created an enormous network of state and municipal theatres and conservatories throughout the country.[36] His recognition of the theatre's contribution to the foundation of the modern state reads like an episode out of *A Thousand and One Nights*:

In 1930, a talented director named Muhsin Ertugrul, who had been active in the municipal theater of Istanbul, brought a troupe of actors to

Ankara and gave ten different plays on ten nights. Busy as Ataturk was with the job of reshaping Turkey, he was there at every performance. When the last curtain fell he summoned Ertugrul into conference with his prime minister. Now, as everyone knew, the maker of modern Turkey was a hard drinker as well as a hard worker, and he said to Ertugrul, 'You have accomplished the impossible. I have been sober for ten evenings. The theatre is what Turkey needs. How can I help you?' Ertugrul replied, 'Give me a school to train new creators.' The liberator woke up his dozing prime minister and said, 'Give this man a school.[37]

Though Ataturk had an unusual respect for actors and their art, the theatre was not free from his nationalist agenda:

The Republic prescribed certain conditions under which creative work would be protected: it must condemn the old regime, glorify nationalism and modernism, promote patriotism, inculcate the ideal of personal sacrifice for the common good.[38]

The Challenge to Bourgeois Theatre

Yildiz Kenter and her brother Musfik Kenter are the pre-eminent couple in the Turkish theatre today. Their long careers span the many political ups and downs that have affected the theatre. Like many of the dramatists whose careers and attitudes were formed by teachers present in the 1950s and 1960s, the Kenters are a part of the Ataturk legacy and his vision of a modern Turkey that gave a clear role for the theatre. In the 1990s, however, they found themselves to be fighting an increasingly uphill battle. Devoted to the theatre for almost half a century, their moral and cultural support from their own society is being subtly eroded.

Originally from Ankara, the Kenters studied at the State Conservatory under the legendary Carl Ebert. Yildiz comments that they had wonderful teachers, many of whom were German Jews. The Kenters worked in the National Theatre in Ankara for eleven years, but in 1959, when the director Muhsin Ertugrul was forced to leave, they also resigned and joined him in Istanbul. In 1961, the Kenters with Ertugrul established the Kent Players. They started to construct their own theatre building and went heavily into

The stage of the Yildiz Palace Theatre in Istanbul, the single remaining court theatre in Turkey.

debt. In order to keep the construction going, they gave over 500 performances in three years, often two performances a day.

In 1968, the Kent Players opened in their new theatre with *Hamlet*, directed by English director Dennis Cary. In the 1960s, Yildiz and her brother played opposite each other in many productions, including *Look Back in Anger* and Ionesco's *The Chairs* and *The Lesson*. In the 1970s, they worked with Russian directors and performed together in most of Chekhov's plays.

For the past eighteen years, they have performed in Istanbul for nine months, taught at the two conservatories in the city, and then toured for two or three months. The cast and staff are becoming increasingly difficult to maintain because the theatre season, which used to extend from 1 October to 30 June, has shrunk by almost two months, and yet the entire staff is kept on an annual salary.

Yildiz remarks that in the past they were able to perform the classics, but in private theatres today comedies are a condition of survival. Even in the past, comedies were used to draw audiences when serious plays were staged – the initial production of *Hamlet* having played alongside a Turkish comedy. But then there was more co-operation from critics in the press to mediate between the performers and their audience. In the current era of commerciality, the Kenters see their major challenge as maintaining high artistic standards while still filling the theatre. 'Without bourgeois theatre', says Yildiz, 'there is no theatre.'[39]

Although Yildiz was quickly noticed as a talented young actress in ensemble work, Musfik Kenter, like Sensoy, initially made a name for himself with monodrama performances as Vincent van Gogh and Clarence Darrow, among others, and some based on the lives of Turkish poets and writers. In 1996 he prepared a one-man show based on Ataturk's address to the nation in 1927. This speech was delivered over the course of five days and rambles in many directions, but Kenter condensed and edited it to present key issues that he felt were particularly pertinent to the times.

'Everyone', he says, 'knows of and reveres Ataturk, but his words have been forgotten. It is time to resurrect the words and remind people of Turkey's destiny as a modern nation.'[40] Ataturk's vision is being lost in the battles between corrupt secular politicians and the Islamic resurgence.

Reflecting Contemporary Instabilities

Yildiz, like her brother, has appeared in many monodramas, her most famous role (both in and outside of Turkey) being a peasant woman in *I, Anatolia*, directed by Haldun Dormen. In 1996, she was preparing a revival of *Latife*, a monodrama of Ataturk's wife of three years. In the same year, both appeared in Refik Erduran's *Ramiz and Julide* (*Ramiz ile Julide*), set during the collapse of Turkey's giant neighbour, the USSR.

With Musfik playing a retired football player and Yildiz an aging porno star, the play exposes the moral exhaustion of the Turkish people, whose moral reserves have been drawn upon and used up. Although the playwright wanted to show the effects of this new source of instability on the psyche of the people, this intention was upstaged by sex. Despite the play's provocative presentation of contemporary problems from an unsubverted Marxist viewpoint, it was a projection on the huge screen which dominated the set of the half-naked Yildiz that had the critics buzzing – and the audiences flocking to the show.

The actress, nonplussed by the 'scandal,' remarked, 'I'm a sixty-six-year-old woman. When I was eleven years old, I played a legendary old mother. Now I play an ex-porn star. *Ramiz and Julide* is one of the most well-written and serious comedies Turkish theatre has produced, yet this is all people pay attention to.'[41] Yet the hoopla proves one of the play's points – that 900-prefix phone numbers (for sexual encounters) have become a way of life in Istanbul: 'This is what people must do now in order to survive.'

While the controversy over Yildiz's breasts raged, the two actors maintained their rigorous teaching schedule. Musfik was directing students in *The Threepenny Opera* at Mimar Sinan Conservatory, while Yildiz was directing Fugard's *Road to Mecca* at Istanbul University. Both student productions were performed in the Kenters' own theatre, since the two conservatories do not have suitable facilities.

Yildiz and her brother complain that their students do not show the same devotion to the theatre that they themselves feel, and that they know is necessary for both the theatre and the actors to survive. Students, they say, are not willing to work as hard and are seduced by thoughts of instant fame on television. 'They do not love the theatre', said Musfik sadly: but Yildiz was still able to find some students, such as the two young women rehearsing *The Road to Mecca*, a source of inspiration

Yildiz was enamoured of this South African play about a liberated old woman who creates statues which all face East toward Mecca, an activity that bemuses and threatens her Christian neighbours. The play reflects the social strain on the creative indi-

Yildiz Kenter directs her students in her production of Athol Fugard's *The Road to Mecca* at the Kenter Theatre.

vidual who persists in harmless activities that are threatening only because they are misunderstood.

The irony of Mecca being the source and inspiration of Miss Helen's creative liberation was not lost on Yildiz. Like Gunsiray's interpretation of Galy Gay as both an Everyman and an artist negotiating his position in a changing society, Fugard's Miss Helen is an eccentric individual motivated by an artistic vision, and if she cannot banish the darkness of the world with a single light, she at least manages to illuminate her own life:

She did something which small minds and small souls can never forgive . . . she dared to be different! . . . Those statues out there *are* monsters. And they are that for the simple reason that they express Helen's freedom. Yes, I never thought it was a word you would like. I'm sure it ranks as a cardinal sin in these parts. A free woman! God forgive us![42]

Yildiz, despite her status as a star, also feels threatened by the pressure of the anonymous masses, who, by their sheer numbers, may defeat individual endeavour.[43]

As committed dramatists, the Kenters deplore what they see as the degradation of the cultural life of Istanbul. 'Art is healthy', says Yildiz, 'like vitamins, but we are being forced to defend and justify ourselves now.' Thus, while they instruct their students with unflagging dedication, instilling into them their own love of theatre, they express a sinking feeling that despite having overcome the vicissitudes of their own careers, they foresee these young people facing an even greater struggle.

The Work of Ahmet Levendoglu

Two other well-known figures in today's Istanbul theatre are Ahmet Levendoglu and Haldun Dormen, who also run their own theatres, and are nurturing the next generation of dramatists. In 1995, Ahmet Levendoglu was instrumental in founding Akademi

Istanbul, a performing arts school that offers an accredited three-year programme in ballet, contemporary dance, music, and theatre. A former teacher at the State Conservatory, Levendoglu became disillusioned with its commercialism – with teachers spending more time on their own careers than teaching students, and students seeking employment rather than learning their craft.

A graduate of RADA, Levendoglu has maintained strong links with British theatre. He chose and translated Terry Johnson's *Hysteria* as the opening production for his troupe – Tiyatro Studyosu – in its own new theatre. The company invested heavily in refurbishing a cinema on the Anatolian side of Istanbul, which, though seating only 370, had a large flexible stage. Work on the theatre encountered many difficulties, but the group felt committed to establishing a theatre on the other side of the Bosphorus.

The play is a serious comedy that examines Freud's theory of infantile seduction, the misreading of female neurosis, and its relation to childhood sexual abuse. The daughter of one of his young female patients returns to the doctor's house at the end of his life to force him to confront the truth of what he had discovered in that case: that it was not the woman's sexual fantasies for her father but her father's abuse that drove her to suicide.

Indeed, Freud came to believe that the sexual desire of fathers for their daughters was so widespread that his own father and he himself were not immune, yet, fearing a backlash against the Jews and himself, he retracted his views. Levendoglu says he chose a play dealing with a sensitive subject because he hoped it would help Turks begin to address the kind of taboo problems that such conservative societies are loath even to acknowledge, let alone discuss.[44]

On 7 March 1996, just three weeks before they were due to open, an electrical accident burned down the theatre. However, the play opened on schedule in Haldun Dormen's theatre, and although the lighting and set had to be adjusted for a smaller stage, the actors gave a taut performance to a very attentive full house.

Haldun Dormen's Boulevard Theatre

Haldun Dormen, the ruling doyen of Istanbul's boulevard theatre, is less satirical than Sensoy, but has been presenting social comedies and farces to sell-out audiences for the past forty years. Starting in the 1950s, Dormen and a few friends created 'Cip' or Pocket Theatre, performing in an apartment space with just 25 seats. Presenting plays by Sartre and Saroyan, 'Cip' was at the time considered very avant garde.[45]

Dormen, the first actor from Istanbul to attend Yale Drama School, surprised his expectant colleagues by staging a farce upon his return. He has continued to direct and act at his own Dormen Theatre, producing Ray Cooney comedies, Feydeau farces, and Neil Simon plays. Like Sensoy, he often adapts foreign plays to a Turkish context. He says Turkish audiences enjoy broad farce as well as the cutting verbal humour often to be found in Jewish plays.

Dormen typically pokes fun at Turkish foibles, such as in his *A Lover's Coming from Germany*, which portrays an Istanbul family whose son awaits the arrival of a German acquaintance recommended by a Turkish friend working in Germany. He imagines a girl in a bikini, but a bearded young man on a bicycle turns up instead. The family's concern over sex is gently satirized. A grandmother who has been kept sequestered all her life imagines the German trying to rape her when he runs after a butterfly.[46]

Dormen teaches comic and music theatre at Istanbul University, and in addition to American musicals has directed a dozen Turkish musicals. In 1996, he was acting in a Turkish adaptation of Feydeau's *A Flea in Her Ear*, translated as *Arapsci*, which literally means 'Arab's hair' but is also the common term for 'maze'. He has also directed the State Theatre using State Opera singers in an extravaganza production of *The King and I*. With a large orchestra and cast, the production was an exceptional success. He felt the audience related to the East–West tensions in the play shown by the King's pride in his own heritage and in his desire for a western education and manners for his children.

Scenes from Tiyatro Studyosu's production of Terry Johnson's *Hysteria*. Top: Freud (Haluk Bilginer), Yehudi (Selim Nasit), Salvador Dali (Mehmet Akan), and Jessica (Zuhal Olcay). Bottom: Dali, Freud, and Yehudi.

Without making any overt reference to a similar duality in the Turkish character, the similarity made the play more poignant than its Hollywood exoticism would suggest. Moreover, Dormen, a thoroughly secular native of Istanbul, emphasized that at the end of the play the king turns again to his traditional posture in prayer, thereby indicating that he does not lose his cultural identity, but returns to tradition as a source of strength compatible with modernization.

Though the spirit of Ataturk may have become dormant in a large part of the population, Istanbul's dramatists seem to feel they have a special reason, even a duty, to revive it. Despite the ascension of Islamist politicians, and the rapid proliferation of religious schools,[47] Ataturk remains a legendary figure of pride for all Turkish people. As Sensoy's Binbela Mahmut demonstrates, the common man still appreciates Ataturk as a national hero even if other personal beliefs are in conflict.

Moreover, as Musfik Kenter suggests, most people have now forgotten the core of Ataturk's message, his secularism having been tainted by the imperfect and often corrupt politicians who have been in power over the past fifteen years. Perhaps with his monodrama Kenter will be able to remind people not only of the leader's dream for the country, but also of the role he saw for theatre.

For, truly, Ataturk was the most devoted advocate of Turkish theatre, and his exhortation to politicians is inscribed in the lobby of Ankara's main theatre: 'Gentlemen, you can all become congressmen or cabinet ministers or even president . . . but you cannot become actors.'[48] Current politicians, secular and Islamist, would both do well to listen to their cultural interpreters in the theatre, and respect Ataturk's insight when he said: 'Drama is the mirror of the cultural level of a country. We should love those who devote their lives to the great art of drama.'[49]

Notes and References

1. The two issues are not unrelated, since the ongoing offensive against the Kurds is draining Turkey's finances, and the Islamist candidates, aside from supporting more religion in public life, have been concerned with practical matters of offering basic amenities to the poor.

2. With the appointment of Refah leader Necmettin Erbakan to the post of Prime Minister, Islamists were likely to gain their biggest share of power in Turkey's modern history. But Turkey's secularist elite, led by the military, opposed Erbakan, whom they feared would replace constitutional law with Koranic law after more than seventy years of secularism, and steer NATO-member Turkey away from the western camp. Though they were able to oust him in 1997, other Refah members throughout the country have held on to their posts. The court decision to outlaw the entire party has incurred a negative response from the United States which suggested that Turkey needed more democratic expression, not less. The political impasse has also impaired Turkey's ability to deal with the thirteen-year-long Kurdish rebel insurgency, its tense relations with Greece over Cyprus, and its deep economic woes. See 'Erbakan Tells Yilmaz: Don't Repeat Mistakes', *Turkish Daily News*, 9 June 1996.

3. In the 1920s (at the beginning of the Republic founded by Mustapha Kemal Ataturk), Turks had been curbed in the practice of their faith. Fulfilment of the duty of pilgrimage to Mecca had become almost impossible. Prayer was in Turkish, not in the Arabic of the Prophet, and theological colleges were closed. But in 1950, as the result of democratic elections, religious education was restored in public schools, and Arabic was reinstated as the language of religion, which pleased rural Anatolians but alienated army officers, educated people, journalists, and students. The government retired judges and dismissed civil servants who opposed the moves, and journalists were imprisoned. After a Kemalist revolution led by a group of army officers in 1959, elections were held in 1960, but coalition governments proved ineffective and the army remained the real power. In the 1960s there was neither a return to Ataturk's anti-clericalism, nor a policy of strengthening religious intervention in public life. Turkey has undergone *coups d'état* in both 1970 and 1980. See Desmond Stewart, *Turkey* (New York: Time, 1965), p. 107.

4. The last major exodus of writers and dramatists from Turkey occurred in 1980 at the time of the military takeover, demonstrating that it is not the Islamists that pose the only threat to freedom of expression. See Petra de Bruijn, 'Turkish Theatre: Autonomous Entity to Multicultural Compound', *Theatre Intercontinental: Forms, Functions, Correspondences*, ed. C. C. Barfoot and Cobi Boredewijk (Amsterdam: Editions Rodopi B.V., 1993), p. 192.

5. Observers of Turkish politics suggest that the success of Islamic candidates does not necessarily threaten to turn Turkey into another Iran or Afghanistan. Polls show that most of Erbakan's supporters simply wanted good and populist government. In her article covering the International Istanbul Theatre Festival in 1997, Elinor Fuchs makes the common American mistake of equating 'Islamist' with 'fundamentalist'. Moreover, she says the Festival was 'facing West' – but modern Turkish theatre and the International Festival have always 'faced West'. See Elinor Fuchs, 'Istanbul Looking West: Art or Politics?', *American Theatre*, XIV, No. 10, p. 40.

6. Yasar Kemal, 'Feldzug der Lugen', *Der Spiegel*, 9 January 1995, p. 134–8.

7. 'A Painful Absurdity', *Turkish Daily News*, 13 April 1996.

8. See 'Kemal Sentence Underlines Double Standards in Turkey', an editorial by the *Turkish Daily News* publisher Ilnur Cevik, in *Turkish Daily News*, 21 March 1996. In 1997 Kemal received a peace prize at the Frankfurt Book Fair, and his sentence has been postponed unless within five years he commits the same crime.

9. Arthur Miller wrote to Kemal, a personal friend: 'In this age, when we send our thoughts anywhere at the touch of a button, you are forbidden, on pain of imprisonment, of letting certain thoughts past your lips. What a painful absurdity! And what power is coiled in this evil seed of suppression that it can be destroyed, so it would seem, in one country [Russia] only to rise on the wind to sprout again in another [Turkey]! If it were not so serious it would be a theme for a comedy, a farce, in fact.' See 'A Painful Absurdity', *Turkish Daily News*, 13 April 1996.

10. David O'Byrne, 'Taking Kafka to Court', *Turkish Daily News*, 25 March 1996.

11. Ibid.

12. Ibid. See also Seventh International Istanbul Theatre Festival programme, p. 100–3.

13. The group's name, meaning 'an ironic joke', was inspired by Musfik Kenter, Turkey's foremost actor and the teacher of many of the Tiyatro Ti actors. Kenter had said, 'Theatre is a serious joke.'

14. Interview with the author, 2 April 1996.

15. A position in the State Theatre is a sinecure for life, which, although it once promised dramatists a measure of security, has now become an obstacle to development and prevents an influx of new talent. The lists are swollen with actors who rarely get on stage and Gunsiray, among others, has been vocal in his criticism of this situation, calling it moribund.

16. Performed in the 250-seat theatre below the Café Marti, a well-known gathering place for artists on Istiklal Caddesi, its audience was more upscale than one might have expected. Young professionals – doctors, lawyers, government workers, as well as dramatists – came during the first week. Performances of small independent troupes are more expensive than those at state or municipal theatres, which are heavily subsidized. Student tickets are especially cheap.

Although newspaper theatre reviews are now scant, with none of the leading papers employing a regular reviewer as they did in the 1960s, Gunsiray's recent notoriety, and news articles discussing the meaning of the play (rather than the performance) aroused the public's curiosity. Devrim Nas, one of the founders of Tiyatro Ti, said, however, that government support for such groups is so minuscule that the members pay for it out of their own pockets, leaving the future of Tiyatro Ti in jeopardy.

17. 'Wrong to Call Nazim Hikmet a Traitor, Says Welfare Party Deputy', *Turkish Daily News*, 15 January 1996.

18. Emre Koyuncuoglu, 'Diyarbakir Belediye Tiyatrosu Kapatildi' ('The Mayor Closed Down the Municipal Theatre of Diyarbakir'), *Tiyatrosu*, November 1995, p. 8–9.

19. The Refah mayor in Ankara, Melih Gokcek, did not like a number of statues in the city, claiming they violated the Islamic law which bans reproduction of the human figure. A sculpture in a public park which abstractly depicts a couple embracing came under fire, but its removal was prevented by a group of outraged artists. The sculptor has brought the case to court. A Hittite sculpture at the entrance to the city, a nationalist and anti-Ottoman symbol since the 1920s, also incited the mayor's displeasure, but rather than approach the subject of its removal directly, it was deemed necessary for the construction of a new overpass. Interview with Sibel Zandi-Sayek, 13 September 1996.

20. In the 1994 municipal elections, many of these new migrant voters protested against the corruption in the ruling party and its lack of concern for their plight, and elected the pro-Islamic Welfare Party candidate, Recep Tayyip Erdogan, as mayor of Istanbul. A former soccer player and civil servant, Erdogan promised to eliminate corruption, provide equitable services to all, and shut down the brothels. It was this promise of social services for the poor that empowered the religious right, since the secularists have ignored this large group for too long. Erdogan installed new water pipelines, new garbage dumps away from the areas in which the poor live, shifted the city to natural gas away from the lignite coal which had been the chief cause of pollution, and created greater incentives to complete the metro system. See 'Islamists in Power', *Turkish Daily News*, 3 June 1996.

21. Interview with author, 4 April 1996. See Eugene Ionesco, *Rhinoceros*, trans. Donald Watson (Harmondsworth: Penguin, 1959), p. 124.

22. Erdinc Ergenc, 'Cultural, Artistic Changes Subtle but Present', *Turkish Daily News*, 1 April 1996.

23. Both Egypt and Iran had lively developing theatres which were directly affected by the change in the political climate: 'The years following the 1967 war with Israel and the assassination of Anwar Sadat in 1981 were not good for the development of Egyptian theatre. Difficult economic conditions during the war years were followed by an upsurge in Islamic religious fundamentalism which made stage productions difficult.

'In Iran, the revolution of 1978–79 stopped much of the theatrical activity that had taken place under the Pahlavi regime, making the future of theatre much less certain. Theatrical training schools and regular performances in public virtually ceased in Iran. National Iranian Radio-Television, its name changed to "The Voice and Vision of the Islamic Republic of Iran", produced dramas on revolutionary themes for television, but stage drama was viewed with great suspicion.' *Cambridge Guide to World Theatre*, ed. Martin Banham (Cambridge University Press, 1988), p. 673–5.

24. Metin And, *A History of Theatre and Popular Entertainment in Turkey* (Ankara: Forum Yayinlari, 1964), p. 11. 'Orthodox Islam in the early period of its existence, categorically forbade the representation of living beings and especially human faces. This ban was generally explained by the fact that Islam aspired to fight idolatry and to fortify monotheism. . . . Moreover, the representation of living beings might seem to the orthodox Moslem an intrusion into the creative activity of God, an imitation of the creatures of Allah.' See also Nicholas N. Martinovitch, *Turkish Theatre* (New York: Theatre Arts, 1933), p. 35–6.

25. Ibid.

26. Martinovitch, op. cit., p. 36.

27. And, op. cit., p. 11.

28. And, op. cit., p. 41.

29. Talat Sait Halman, *Modern Turkish Drama* (Minneapolis: Bibliotheca Islamica, 1976), p. 18.

30. During the past few years, the one time of the year that the more secular-leaning dramatists make use of Ottoman theatre traditions is during the holy month of Ramadan. Merih Tangun, a teacher at Mimar Sinan, says that during Ramadan it is popular 'to go back to one's roots'. Interview with the author, 3 April 1996.

31. Rengin Uz, 'Feleck Bir Gun Salakken' ('One Day When Fate Was Stupid'), *Tiyatrosu*, March 1996, p. 22.

32. Brecht has been a favourite author with Turkish dramatists since the 1960s. His epic theatre has also been particularly embraced by some actors and troupes, such as the Dostlar Tiyatro. Fuchs comments on the dominance of the German presence at the International Festival and the success of the Berliner Ensemble's performance of *The Resistible Rise of Arturo Ui*. Zeliha Berksoy, a German-trained Brecht advocate and actress with the State Theatre, suggests that Brecht especially suits the Turkish temperament. 'Brecht liked the Mediterranean peoples. The Germans perform his works with a harsh edge, but the Turks and their southern European neighbours give his plays a softer, more languid style.'

Berksoy, herself the daughter of a famous opera singer, regularly performs Brecht/Weill songs. She suggests that Brecht offers something familiar in style to the traditional Turkish theatre, *orta oyunu*, so that audiences and actors alike relate to it, even if unconsciously. Although Brecht's plays were most popular in the 1960s and he is now somewhat out of fashion, she feels his work takes on additional poignancy in the 1990s because of the rise of a yuppy-style entreprenurism and political corruption. Interview with author, 3 April 1996.

Only one Brecht play has ever been prevented from opening, when, in 1960, the Municipal Theatre was forbidden to play *Good Woman of Setzuan* because of the Moslem interdiction against representation of the gods.

The Threepenny Opera had already inspired a Turkish adaptation, *The Ballad of Ali of Keshan*, by Haldun Taner, which Sensoy has directed at the Istanbul Municipal Theatre in 1988, and which has been translated into English. See de Bruijn, op. cit., for the history of Brecht production in Turkey.

33. Programme, Seventh International Istanbul Theatre Festival, p. 61–3.

34. Concerned about the development of new buildings destroying Istanbul's famous skyline of minarets and domes, Sensoy wrote *Istanbul for Sale*, which was translated into English in 1991.

35. In the Turkish Constitution of 1961, wider freedoms were enacted, enabling playwrights to deal with social and economic problems in less guarded or allegorical terms, bringing to the stage a whole spectrum of political themes and tensions. By the end of the decade over thirty plays were being offered on any given day in Istanbul and Ankara. (See Halman, op. cit., p. 38–40.) Macgowan and de Bruijn, too, expressed astonishment at the breadth of theatrical offerings in Istanbul during the 1960s. The quantity and range is still impressive in the 1990s, with up to twenty different productions a week.

36. The introduction and growing popularity of European theatre occurred in the mid-nineteenth century. Concerned that western troupes would dominate, the mayor of Istanbul, Cemil Pasha, started a conservatory of music and theatre in 1914. Called Darulbedayi i Osmani, this was headed first by André Antoine, who returned to France at the outbreak of war, the conservatory then being directed by Muhsin Ertugrul. Darulbedayi gave its first performance – *Rotten Foundations* by Emile Fabre, adapted by Huseyin Suat – in 1916, and became the Istanbul City Theatre in 1931. With both the City Theatre and the foundation of state theatres in Ankara and Istanbul in 1940, the promotion and production of Turkish plays was guaranteed. See Deniz Taskan, *Theatre in Turkey* (Ankara: Directorate General of Press and Information, 1993), p. 4–5.

Turkey never developed a specific style of court theatre. The court interest in western theatre helped to promote it in the city for the general public. The small theatre in the Yildiz Palace, Istanbul, is the only extant court theatre in Turkey. Built by Sultan Abdulhamit II in 1889, it hosted many European luminaries such as Sarah Bernhardt – whom, however, the Sultan refused to watch, because she acted death scenes too effectively. See Halman, op. cit., p. 36.

37. Kenneth Macgowan, 'Notes on Turkish Theatre', *Drama Survey*, No. 3 (Winter 1962), p. 322.

38. Stewart, op. cit., p. 119. In addition to the municipal and state theatre system, Ataturk created Halkevleri, or 'people's houses' for community cultural projects and education. Five hundred were established in the 1930s, and inspired the formation of many theatre companies, but President Menderes dismantled the Halkevleri in the 1950s.

39. Interview with author, 5 April 1996.

40. Ibid.

41. Rengin Uz, 'Ciddi Bir Komedi Oynuyoruz' ('It's a Serious Comedy'), *Tiyatrosu*, December 1995, p. 52–6.

42. Athol Fugard, *Road to Mecca* (New York: Theatre Communications Group, 1985), p. 60–1.

43. Fuchs correctly intuits that Kenter's performance of Maria Callas in *The Master Class* was a vehicle to express a 'political statement about the transcendent role of art in human culture', similar to the actress's own view. See Fuchs, op. cit., p. 42.

44. Interview with author, 5 April 1996. Tiyatro Studyosu won acclaim with its premiere of Turgay Nar's *Garbage Dump* shown at the Seventh Istanbul International Theatre Festival, 1995. Set in the Middle Ages, the play is a poetical allegory of contemporary quandaries and sense of displacement.

45. Interview with author, 4 April 1996, and interview with Ambassador Yuksel Soylemez, Taipei, 26 April 1996.

46. Stewart, op. cit., p. 120.

47. The government has put an end to their increase by mandating an extension of compulsory public education.

48. Halman, op. cit., p. 38.

49. Quoted in programme for the Seventh International Istanbul Theatre Festival.

Joanna Rotté

Feldenkrais Revisited: Tension, Talent, and the Legacy of Childhood

Moshe Feldenkrais developed his influential philosophy and physiology of movement from a background in engineering, and a concern to remedy a knee injury sustained in a game of soccer. Though he scorned psychoanalytical approaches to the remedying of poor or painful postures, he had great faith in the capacity of the body, through the brain, for self-correction and self-healing. Joanna Rotté met Feldenkrais shortly before his death in 1985, in his eightieth year, and talked to him during a nine-week course he was leading in his own methodology. Joanna Rotté now teaches Script Analysis and Voice and Movement at Villanova University, outside Philadelphia. Her travel memoir *Scene Change*, a theatre diary from Prague, Moscow, and Leningrad, was published by Limelight in 1994, and her performance piece, *Death of the Father*, was produced in the spring of 1998 at the National Museum of Women in the Arts in Washington, D.C.

A FEW YEARS *before he died in 1985, in his eightieth year, I interviewed Moshe Feldenkrais on the campus of Hampshire College in Amherst, Massachusetts, where he was conducting a nine-week teacher-training programme in Feldenkrais methodology. The path that led an engineer to arrive at the role of an internationally respected specialist in movement is useful to review. It began during his teenage years in Tel Aviv where he practised jujitsu and played soccer, and continued in Paris where he studied both electrical and mechanical engineering as well as taking a doctorate in physics at the Sorbonne.*

An old soccer injury flared up, chronic knee pain began to set in, and it was to this problem that Feldenkrais applied his technical and scientific knowledge combined with studies in neurophysiology. During the Second World War he escaped to London, working as a scientist and conducting classes in judo. As his teaching developed, he included yoga-like postures and exercises to explore the functioning of antagonistic muscle groups in relation to gravity. His research convinced him that all the injuries in a person's life – physical, psychological, emotional – are captured in the physical body; and that this history gets written into the muscles and the patterns of their use.

From the Feldenkrais perspective, it is unnecessary, in the interest of self-healing, to retrace

one's past through psychoanalysis. A person can be released from their past, including past injuries, by changing their pattern of movement. This entails releasing habitual patterns of distorted muscular use (since injury causes muscular distortion) and then finding comfortable movement through awareness.

During the years of his work as a renowned practitioner, Feldenkrais assisted two kinds of pupils – as he preferred to call them, since his stated approach was not medicinal but educational. There were the extraordinary pupils suffering from multiple sclerosis or cerebral palsy, on whom he practised a method of manipulation called functional integration; and there were the ordinary pupils to whom he taught awareness exercises for increasing brain use, based on his claim that the average person uses only five to ten per cent of brain capacity. 'What I'm after', he said, 'isn't flexible bodies but flexible brains.' It is these awareness exercises to which the theatre and performing arts communities have been drawn.

When I met Feldenkrais, his posture and carriage appeared comfortable. His shoulders looked relaxed. His gait was like a broom, kept close to the floor. He wore black cotton trousers in martial arts style and a blousey white, Indian-influenced shirt on a not tall but sturdy frame. On his feet were black Chinese-like cloth shoes. His own

351

being modelled his intention: 'To restore each person to their human dignity.'

I asked him to speak to his practice of getting at the mind through the body: why this emphasis on using movement to teach the body to re-programme the brain?

Every actor knows the essentiality of movement. The important thing about movement is: can he walk? Can he stand by himself? Can she go to the toilet by herself? Can she see to the right and the left? Can she hear? In other words, as far as movement goes, how can you imagine life without it? Obviously, it's the most general thing and the most important capacity for any person. A person who doesn't move at all – if he doesn't breathe and has no heartbeat, no regurgitating, and no defecation – surely he is dead.

Your teaching is addressed to the average person, to increase or heighten his or her awareness through movement. But the average person can already walk and stand and turn. . . .

Oh, that's what he thinks!

Perhaps not well. . . .

It's not a question of 'well'. I'm not interested in anybody walking well. I'm interested in him. A person comes to me and says, 'My posture is bad', or he comes and says, 'My breathing is bad.' People come. I never ask them. I have never told anyone, 'You have a bad posture and your eyes are cockeyed and your head is tilted.' It's not my business.

So, the average person can believe that his posture is all right but can get to work, can improve their feeling about their posture. Your *feeling*, that's all. Your posture must change in such a way that it becomes to you a good feeling. Do you feel your breathing is as perfect as you want? Is your eyesight good?

My eyesight is not so good, but my breathing is all right.

Well, there you are. If you ask people, they'll say, 'My voice is not so good.' People complain. The average person complains. If the average person were feeling well, he wouldn't be doing any jogging. There are

millions of people jogging in America. Why do they jog?

To feel better.

Because they feel bad. They feel they're clumsy. And, by the way, their jogging is not that good either. There are few people who jog and improve. So there is a question about jogging. Is your swimming perfect? Can you swim as well as Mark Spitz?

No.

Why not? You're an average person.

Insufficient training.

Training only? There are plenty of people who train to swim and none swims like Mark Spitz.

Insufficient desire.

The average person gives it up! So you see, the average person is actually the most interesting person, because none or very few of the 4.5 billion average people are satisfied with their own being. But average men and women are too silly to understand all their problems. They have their trouble, and they either just keep it to themselves or they go into psychotherapy. Or they read books about holistic health and try to do something by themselves, or they go to practitioners of the dozens of different healing methods taught.

So the average person is actually aware that he is not doing justice to his own make-up, to his potential. He feels that he could be better. So, you see, it is not I who wants the average person to be well, to get his posture straight. I don't know what straight means for him. If I make your posture the way I like it, you will find it awful. I must make your posture the way that *feels to you* to be the posture you'd like to feel.

Is that what you mean when you speak of a correct self-image for each person?

Yes, each person has his own make-up.

And the correct image cannot come from outside oneself?

No, it cannot. Because if it could, a person would have it.

Will there always be some conflict within a person between the society's image of what he should be and his own personally correct self-image?

In our society, in our culture, it is unavoidable. But some anthropologists have found a very few, very small communities in the world where it isn't like this. They haven't got the big problems of big countries where the solutions are not simple.

So your way for a person to reach his correct self-image is through action?

Yes, because without action we can't know what we would like to feel.

And you teach that one of the crucial factors contributing to a person's getting away from his correct self-image is the experience of pain.

Yes, most of the problems people have come through pain, whether it is tooth pain, eye pain, neck pain, ear pain, stomach pain.

Or social pain? Or pain from one's parents?

Yes, emotional pain – deep insults to a child, let us say, who loses all confidence and does not consider himself worthy of standing on his own feet.

But how do I know when I'm manifesting my correct self-image?

Actually, to say the word correct is not correct. Can you see? Knowing this in itself actually helps you already to understand that you are not going to be given a series of rules: that you would have to hold your head like this, your hand like that, and your feet like this, and then you would be all right. That would be cuckoo, wouldn't it?

If I want to help you to feel comfortable in your mind, I must bring you to a state that you feel is correct for you. The state you are brought to must be one which makes you a more effective person with more direct performance of your intention. You must be helped to get to a state where you have a good nervous system but do not need to know that you have a nervous system.

For example, if you want to take a good look at me, you take it. At this point, you don't need to know that you have a nervous system. You only need to focus and press a sight button. But if another person wants to take a good look at me and he has a tremor in his neck, then he knows that he has a tremor and a nervous sytem, and he would go to a neurologist to find out what's wrong with his nervous system. In other words, a well-organized nervous system is one you don't know you have.

The nervous system that works healthily makes it so that whatever you intend to do – through your internal drive or as a reaction to something happening outside of you – is performed easily, comfortably, with elegance, and doesn't take five movements in order to perform one action. My objective is to educate the person so much about himself that he doesn't find any more fault with himself. But if a person sits like this (*slumping forward*), and if I talk to him for ten years telling him to sit straight, he can't do it. He wouldn't know what I mean.

So how does a person become aware? You can start just by stretching out your arms and looking at their length in front of you. Which arm is longer? So, you may say, 'That one's longer.' Now, would you want to make it shorter? Or can you make the shorter one longer? So, if I adjust your head: now, see, the shorter one's gotten longer. So, I may say, 'Look, if adjusting your head makes the shorter arm longer, maybe you actually hold your head to the other side all the time, and that's why the arm on that side is longer.

Since that is so, you will find that you move your head only to one side and that the other side is stiff in the neck and doesn't move at all. Now, how come, if you're an average healthy person? Where did you learn to move your head to one side and not to the other?' And you may say, 'I always had one eye better than the other.' And I will say, 'Oh, yeah? Is it your eyes? All right, let's close the eyes and see.' And you'll find that if you move the eyes slowly to the stiff side, your stiff neck will move.

Now let's see what this man does if I tell him to get up from the chair. See, he gets up using this side because he sits on this side. He can get up only on this leg, only on this side. So, I'll say, 'How would you get up on the other side? How would you do that?' Then he will find, in trying to get up on the other side, that he doesn't sit on the other hip at all. Because his head is tilted or twisted. He doesn't know that I can put this book in there under the side he doesn't sit on, but that I cannot slide the book under the hip he does sit on.

In other words, the average man in the street comes with a minor problem – like, he holds his shoulder up. When you look closer, you can see that it took a very extraordinary machine – a human brain – and circumstances of his childhood, and misunderstanding of his teachers and parents, to make that child into a being that found it was easier to be cockeyed. When he discovers that his posture is not good, he suddenly realizes the harm he has been doing to himself. His bad posture is because he has not been aware of how he has been standing, sitting, walking, holding himself. He has been cockeyed from longstanding habit.

Let's say, for example, if one side of the pelvis is raised and so the opposite shoulder is also raised so as to achieve balance –

Yes, it can't be otherwise.

Well, does it matter to you where the imbalance started, if it started in the pelvis or in the shoulder?

It never started in the pelvis or in the shoulder. It started in the brain, wherever or whatever it is.

So you are not interested in correcting this part or that part of the body?

I am not interested in correcting anybody or any part of anybody. I'll tell you something (*touching the tip of his thumb to the tip of his little finger*) – you'll find that this is a peculiarly human thing. No animal can do this. No ape can do this, because the ape's thumb is here on the side. Now, try to separate my fingers. If you cannot touch and hold these fingers together, you are certainly not using

your full human capacity, your ability of carrying out an intention to perform. If you go into a mental hospital and find people far gone with schizophrenia, you will find few of them who can hold these fingers together. The people who can are those who have got the ability to intend and to do, which means to act normally. If I want to get up, I get up. But if somebody wants to get up and takes a half-hour, that's a nervous system which is what?

Weak.

The average person uses about ten per cent of his ability.

Do you think diet is a contributory factor in the development of a person's awareness?

Certainly. If you take poison, it contributes.

Is poison different for each person?

There are some poisons that will kill anybody – a few drops of cyanide will do that. But the diet has an influence undoubtedly.

Quantity? Quality?

Both. Quantity, certainly. Quality, certainly. Try eating rotten tomatoes for a week and you will see that quality makes a difference.

There's a saying in China that at the moment of birth it is already too late to begin childhood education.

That is certainly true. Because when children come out into the world, they can already hear. In a few hours or a few days, they can already see. They can already sweat and cry. Where did they learn that? They learned it in the womb. Otherwise, how could a baby breathe coming out? He's in water. He comes out and then on the first contact with air he makes the primal cry and exhales and takes in air. Obviously he has already been having training to perform that.

In fact, we now know that children are actually taking into the lungs some amniotic liquid and regurgitating it. When they come out, the water is thrown out and the air is then taken in, and that starts respiration. The lungs have learned elasticity, everything has been formed, there is already haemoglobin, and the blood is coming through absorbing oxygen and exuding carbon dioxide.

What about artistic awareness or consciousness? How is that developed?

You know, the eunuchs were known to have made a nice choir, with strong but feminine voices. Sopranos. And their musical compositions were Vatican property and were never published. So nobody knew the music. But we know that Liszt was in the Vatican and he listened, and he went home and wrote down the music. It's said that Mozart could do the same thing.

So some few people can listen to a long drawn-out hymn or service or composition and then go home and write it down in musical notation. But many people can't even remember a tune, or can only remember da-da-da-*da* of the whole Ninth Symphony. But there was that extraordinary musical awareness of a Beethoven who could write when he was deaf. Of course, consciousness and awareness and being awake are three different things.

How does talent enter into this? Do you consider talent to be evidence of an inborn inclination or of a developed ability?

If you can discover talent at the age of three days and tell me that *this* child is going to be a general and that *that* child is going to be a mathematician, then I will know what talent means. We talk about talent once it's there, not before. No one could have said fifty or even twenty years ago that I would be doing awareness through movement training or giving lectures. So, is this a talent? What do we mean by a talent? Somebody is a talented musician. At what point did he become a talented musician?

I'm uncertain of the moment, but an attraction to music must have always been there. The talented musician must have originally been drawn to music as a form of expression. He must have liked music and felt comfortable with it and that he could develop a facility for it.

When does someone discover that?

When is the talent called a talent? It seems that would be an acknowledgement coming from the outside. Someone knowledgeable sees the talent and names it.

Can you destroy it?

Probably not entirely.

Talent is a word that grown-up people have found to describe a quality once it's there and everyone knows that it's there. Therefore, talent is not an inborn thing.

Are you saying that talent comes from what a child is exposed to in the environment?

It's not an inborn thing. The only inborn thing is tissues and a brain that's capable of learning. The talent is inculcated. You cannot be a talented pianist without ten or twenty years of playing music at a piano. You can only say that to be talented at something you must be interested in it. Because if you are not interested in music, you won't have the patience or won't find the time to practice some ten hours every day as many talented pianists need to do.

Is it conceivable that someone could grow up in some backward country without any musical instrument and at the age of sixteen go out and look for a piano? Or do you think for a person to become a musician there has to be already a piano in the home when he's growing up?

If somebody hadn't learned Chinese before the age of sixteen, he wouldn't ever learn it unless he were living in China or needed to know the language. It's the same thing with the piano. If an Eskimo was born in an igloo and never heard of or saw a piano in his life, and then you brought him at the age of sixteen to the Juilliard, you would see that no teacher there would undertake to teach him. The teacher would think it's a waste of time. And why should the Eskimo play the piano?

But if he were seven years old, would it be different?

No. For an Eskimo to be brought to the Juilliard at the age of seven, it's too late. An

Eskimo child being brought to the Juilliard and seeing these people fiddling, and those others playing brass, and others drumming, he would just be driven crazy. He would find himself running away, saying, 'They're a band of mad people.'

Yet he could be very musical. He could detect the movement of a white bear on the ice that all of Juilliard would never detect. He wouldn't be called a talented musician, yet if he'd been born here he could have been a musician. And by the way, if you think about this a little bit, does a talented musician also not have to have somewhere in his guts a desire for the public to hear him? And why does a talented musician want a public? Why can't he learn to play the piano and go to the seashore and play for himself?

He desires the performance. He wants that public contact.

A talented pianist must have an audience that can understand that talented pianist. Otherwise, he wouldn't be able to sustain the capacity to practise for ten years. For what? And who would build pianos if there were not a public interested in hearing the piano? When somebody can play so that the public is interested, he then has the potential to develop into a genius – and be given a lot of money, and so on. A pianist needs that.

And he needs an audience.

In an Eskimo child there is no sense of that need for an understanding public. He would not comprehend what you wanted for him with the piano, why he should torture himself ten hours a day – unless you introduce him to the public, and educate him, and make him into a western child. At seven years, its's too late. You will have to bring in a lot of psychiatrists, and they would not know what to do with the child.

What do you think of the Hindu concept of karma, of a former life having some influence on what a person becomes in this life?

I don't believe it. I don't deal with things I don't know. I don't go into things that are impossible to know, that I have no means of knowing. I know about as much as you do about things that are impossible to know. I also know as much as people who claim that they know, but they don't know either.

What about the effects of heredity?

Heredity can be quite well defined. Heredity means that if you were born in Japan to natives of that country, then your eyes are Japanese.

You don't mean that heredity is just physiological?

Not only physiological. The tissues of the brain are also involved. There is the quality of the brain: the way it can learn, how much it can learn, what sort of retention it has. That's all heredity.

What role do parents play in who the child becomes?

What can I say? If we didn't have parents, we would be all right. But if you think about it, most parents are actually much better than not. They have two or three cuckoo things that they do to their children, things they do wrongly. And generally they don't do them wrongly intentionally. They themselves are probably a bit cuckoo, having been wronged by somebody else before.

How many wrong things can a mother do to a child? Or tell a child? 'Be careful', or 'Don't do that, you silly', or something. She can have fifteen faults in her behaviour. But do you know what it takes to bring a person to the age of twenty? How many sleepless nights did she have with that baby having its thumb there, its teeth, diarrhoea, and childhood diseases? And she managed to get it to school and clothe it. Even if you get bad parents, the badness is one per cent of what they do good. But that one per cent can be just like putting a spoonful of sand in a Rolls Royce. The spoonful of sand can spoil the Rolls Royce. That's parents.

Neil Blackadder

Dr. Kastan, the Freie Bühne, and Audience Resistance to Naturalism

An acknowledged feature of the late nineteenth-century reinvigoration of theatre is the frequency with which new styles of writing – and, more often, innovative themes – affronted the public, both in print and performance. Yet the turbulent initial audience reactions to taboo- and ground-breaking plays have often been represented as self-evident confrontations between progressive creative artists and philistine theatregoers. By closely examining one apparently typical case of resistance to the new drama – the uproar at the 1889 premiere in Berlin of Gerhart Hauptmann's *Before Sunrise* – Neil Blackadder demonstrates the complex relationship between production and reception in the early modern theatre. He considers the behaviour of one offended spectator in particular, along with the response of the independent theatre society which staged the production, and a court's verdict on the validity of his protests. Beyond marking an important turning-point in the history of German theatre, the premiere of *Before Sunrise* encapsulates several key facets of the modern theatre during a period when its practitioners were becoming more bold and experimental, while changing norms of conduct were, paradoxically, rendering audiences more restrained. Neil Blackadder is Assistant Professor of the Practice of Drama at Duke University, curently visiting at Knox College. He is writing a book on modern theatre scandals.

A CURIOUS CASE came before a Berlin court in the winter of 1889–90. The recently formed Verein Freie Bühne, Germany's first independent theatre society, had taken legal action against one of its members in an effort to compel him to leave the organization. The board of the Freie Bühne wanted to expel Doctor Isidor Kastan because of his behaviour during one performance, but he refused to surrender his membership card. So the court's task was to decide whether or not the organization had adequate grounds for his expulsion.

On the face of it, nothing more was at stake in this case than one individual's membership of a small organization. Yet Dr. Kastan's actions, along with the responses of the theatre society and the court, compose a revealing picture of the attitudes and assumptions which informed both the production and the reception of the new drama at a particularly important period in European theatre history.

The performance in question was the premiere at Berlin's Lessingtheater, on a Sun-day afternoon in October 1889, of Gerhart Hauptmann's first play, *Vor Sonnenaufgang* (*Before Sunrise*). Several weeks earlier, the Freie Bühne had staged Ibsen's *Ghosts* as its opening production – a play which of course had provoked a great deal of controversy throughout Europe; but by 1889 the theatre-going public was familiar with Ibsen's play, and the Freie Bühne's production was well received. The premiere of *Before Sunrise*, on the other hand, a new play by a young German author, turned into a famously tumultuous occasion. This is how a contemporary reviewer described the audience's response:

The battles between enthusiasm and disapproval, bravos and boos, hissing and clapping, the heckling, the demonstrations, the unrest, the excitement, all of which followed each act, indeed burst in on the action, transformed the theatre into a meeting place filled with a passionate, heaving mob.[1]

The work that caused such uproar is now generally recognized as the first German Naturalist play to have been staged. Up until

357

then Naturalism had been advocated as the means to reinvigorate German theatre, but not yet practised. In the late 1880s, theatre in Berlin was thriving as a business but stagnating as an art form: the repertoire consisted primarily of a few tried and tested German and French authors and their lacklustre imitators; the Prussian authorities practised strict censorship; and the highly competitive market led theatre managers to back reliable successes rather than to take any risks.

Naturalist theatre grew out of the desire of a few mostly liberal-minded intellectuals to replace the dominant form of drama, based on conventions and artifice, with a theatre of 'truthfulness' and 'representation of life'.[2] In an essay of 1891, Otto Brahm – the chairman of the Freie Bühne – took the French society drama as the epitome of all that the Naturalists opposed, and argued that the 'society drama [*Gesellschaftsstück*] is the enemy of Naturalism in content and form. It fabricates a world which does not exist: in which one loves and does not starve.'[3] But in the late 1880s the majority of theatregoers certainly expected and apparently wished to watch characters loving and not starving; and the general perception of Naturalism was of a movement of extremists who aimed to fill the theatres with depressing plays about the vice and depravity of the proletariat.

If the would-be literary revolutionaries were to change the state of German theatre, they had to circumvent a situation which rendered innovation virtually impossible. The Verein Freie Bühne finally provided a means of doing so. Modelled in part on Antoine's Théâtre Libre in Paris, the Freie Bühne was founded in April 1889 by a group of young writers along with a publisher and a lawyer. The organization did not present itself as a Naturalist project, but just as Naturalism needed the Freie Bühne to break through into the mainstream of German drama, the Freie Bühne needed a German Naturalist play to make a real impression on the theatrical climate in Berlin. The virtually unknown 26-year-old Gerhart Hauptmann provided just such a play in *Before Sunrise*, which scandalized and polarized the public well before the premiere.

'Before Sunrise' and the Berlin Public

Before Sunrise was published in mid-August 1889, and Hauptmann and his publisher embarked on a publicity drive which succeeded in bringing the play to the attention of a considerable segment of Berlin society. Paul Schlenther – one of the founders of the Freie Bühne – claimed that 'within a fortnight half of Berlin had read the play'.[4] This publicity guaranteed the play a large readership, but not an impartial one. *Before Sunrise* became the centre of a 'wild whirlpool of persistent rumours'.[5] No doubt word-of-mouth accounts emphasized and exaggerated certain aspects of the play and neglected others. As Paul Schlenther put it: 'It was not the literary merit of the book which prompted people to read it, but its Naturalistic content.'[6] *Before Sunrise* corresponded closely to the public perception of Naturalism as a movement which dwelled on the sordid and preached socialist doctrine.

Otto Brahm and his colleagues on the board of the Freie Bühne quickly decided to produce *Before Sunrise*. And in a further indication of the strong adverse reaction of part of the public, during the rehearsal period some of the actors received outraged and threatening anonymous letters.

Before Sunrise is set in rural Silesia, where the would-be social reformer Loth looks up Hoffmann, a friend from university, who has become a *nouveau riche* by marrying into a landowning family, the Krauses, and mercilessly taking advantage of the local peasants and miners. Frau Krause, stepmother to Hoffmann's wife Martha and to Helene, is having an affair with Kahl – her nephew and Helene's fiancé. Krause is 'always the last guest to leave the inn',[7] and his whole family and circle are depicted as alcoholics, except Helene, who falls in love with the visitor Loth, a proselytizing teetotaller.

Loth returns Helene's love, until Doctor Schimmelpfennig enlightens him about the alcoholism in her family, which disqualifies her as a potential wife for the principled

Loth. He decides to flee, leaving Helene a hastily-written note. When she finds it, she commits suicide.

At noon on Sunday 20 September, the already controversial play finally came before an audience. Many descriptions of that afternoon compare it to a battle, as two sides faced off:

The excited 'Jüngstdeutschen' came into the theatre as if they were going into battle. For them it was now a matter of using hands and feet to clap and stamp victory for the Naturalist view of art. But the opponents' troops were ready for battle too.[8]

Yet this colourful description is probably misleading in its suggestion that most of the spectators intended to fight for one side or the other. According to one review, the auditorium was filled mainly with 'Berlin's old first-night audience, made up of brokers, lawyers, civil servants, roués, and women of the bourgeoisie and the demi-monde, who applaud smutty farces at the Residenz-Theater and venerable classics at the Schauspielhaus with the same pleasure'.[9] It is clear from the various accounts of the premiere that many spectators did not know the play beforehand, and were not necessarily predisposed to oppose or support it. But Dr. Kastan certainly was ready for battle.

Dr. Kastan's Disruptive 'Script'

Kastan figured prominently in the colourful display of varied and impassioned audience reactions, making his opposition to Hauptmann's play especially clear at three points. In Act Two a series of incidents is depicted which revolve around sexuality: Krause, in a drunken stupor, gropes his own daughter Helene; Kahl emerges half-dressed from Frau Krause's room and bribes the farm-hand Beibst not to tell anyone he has seen him; Frau Krause fires Marie, a maid who has been sleeping with one of the other servants; and Helene warns her stepmother that if she does send Marie away she will tell everyone that Frau Krause is sleeping with Kahl.

At some point during or right after this final scene, Dr. Kastan shouted the rhetorical question: 'Sind wir hier in einem Bordell oder in einem Theater?' ('Are we in a brothel here or a theatre?'). This outburst instantly changed the focus of the controversy from the stage to the auditorium, and brought about a reversal: those who had previously hissed at the play applauded him, while those who had applauded the play hissed at him.[10]

Act Four centres on a lengthy love scene between Loth and Helene, during which Kastan emitted a 'heartless burst of laughter'[11] intended to induce the spectators to join him in protesting against the frequent hugs and kisses. But Kastan found no support: 'In a trice the laugher was made to shut up.'[12]

During the fifth and final act, Hoffmann's wife is in labour upstairs, and the characters on stage talk about her progress. At one point the script calls for her 'moaning' to be audible, but this detail was omitted from the first production.[13] Nevertheless, Kastan had read the play, and came prepared: at some point he stood up, removed from his jacket a large pair of forceps, and held them up as if to offer them to the doctor on stage. Since Kastan was sitting in the stalls, the majority of the spectators noticed this supplement to the action on stage. Indeed, one memoir records that for some time afterwards people in Berlin referred to obstetrical forceps as *Kastanietten*.[14]

Undoubtedly the gesture with the forceps and probably also the cry of 'Are we in a brothel?' were premeditated, scripted by Kastan; and even his vain attempt to protest against the love-scene may well have been planned. He seized on three passages in the text and performed his opposition to them, casting himself in the role of spokesman for spectators who would not allow reprehensible use of the stage to pass unchallenged. The scenes which Kastan disrupted most successfully highlight sexuality and childbirth – topics which according to prevailing mores ought to have been kept confined within strict boundaries.

However, the general audience response to *Before Sunrise* demonstrates that not all Kastan's objections to the play were shared by the majority of the spectators. The failure of Kastan's effort to incite a derisive reaction to Act Four suggests the capacity of a well-written and sensitively performed love scene to win over its audience, regardless of the antipathy they might have felt towards the play as a whole, or towards either or both of the lovers.

Act Three centres on a heated conversation between the socialist-orientated Loth and the conservative, self-serving Hoffmann, during which many of the spectators expressed their hostility towards Loth: 'The tirades of the shallow starry-eyed idealist Loth . . . were followed by scornful laughter.'[15] None the less, it appears that during the next act everyone in the audience excepting Kastan became thoroughly engaged by the same character's romantic *tête-à-tête* with Helene.

Theatre or Brothel?

Little more than a week after the performance, the board of the Freie Bühne sent an announcement to the members of the society, informing them that 'in response to complaints received by the board, as well as our own observations, we have expelled a gentleman who with the preconceived intention of disturbing the peace during the second performance by the organization, provoked the outrage of those in his immediate and distant vicinity through offensive words and behaviour'.[16] To Kastan himself, the Freie Bühne sent a sum of money equivalent to his membership dues, along with the request that he return his membership card. Kastan refused to accept his expulsion, returning the letter unopened, and the Freie Bühne thereupon began legal proceedings against him.

While the statement by the board makes no distinction between Kastan's two principal disruptions of the performance, the decision handed down by the court discusses and rules on them separately (his failed attempt to interrupt Act Four was not considered). With regard to the cry, 'Are we in a brothel?', the court judged this 'an utterance that did not go beyond the right of defence'.[17]

They reached this conclusion through a consideration of the particular situation of performances by an independent theatre society – of productions not requiring a licence because they are open only to the paying members of the organization. The court points out that utterances during the performance by Kastan or by any other members of the Freie Bühne

cannot be judged according to what is permitted at ordinary theatrical performances, because in those cases the audience is protected by the authorities against attacks on its views of propriety and morals, whereas here it must protect itself.[18]

Thus the fact that Kastan supplanted the play and made himself the centre of attention was a direct consequence of the very mode of existence of the Freie Bühne: the corollary to an independent theatre society's circumvention of censorship was that it had to accept a greater freedom of expression on the part of its audience.

What the court does not address in judging Kastan's disruption of Act Two is the form of his protest. After all, he did not simply yell 'This is digusting!' or 'Shouldn't be allowed!', as plenty of other spectators did.[19] Instead he staged a small performance of his own, shouting 'Are we in a brothel or a theatre?' not because he sought an answer to his question but in order to draw attention to the discrepancy between *Before Sunrise* and theatre as usually practised.

Kastan reminded his fellow spectators that the only place where one would expect to encounter lewd sexuality and adultery was the brothel; yet one might argue that in doing so he underlined and exacerbated the alleged offensiveness of the play. The court did not read it this way, but focused on Kastan's right, as a member of an independent theatre society, to protest by whatever means he saw fit against a misuse of the theatrical medium. The court's judgment of Kastan's interjection suggests that, according to their model of attack and defence, or offence and defence, whereby spectators had to protect themselves against assaults by an uncensored performance, any tactics were justifiable.

The court's decision does indicate why *Before Sunrise* would have been perceived as an 'attack on the audience's views'. Kastan's assessment of Act Two is endorsed by the court when they mention, as if this were an indisputable feature of the script, the play's 'crude offensiveness'.[20] The decision refers to a law which 'makes impossible the public performance of a play in which situations such as precede or follow sexual intercourse are concretely brought into view, because according to our morals such representations cause offence.'[21] (This paraphrase of the law does not concern itself with the depiction of intercourse itself, presumably because it was taken for granted that simulating actual sex was so far out of bounds as to be unimaginable.)

For authorities in Wilhelmine Germany, and for all those well-to-do citizens whose interests they represented, certain subjects were suitable for dramatic representation before the public and others were not. Act Two of *Before Sunrise* actually includes two unmistakably post-coital scenes, and all the accounts of the premiere make clear that the majority of the audience felt and expressed growing revulsion as the act proceeded. A prominent bourgeois critic, Isidor Landau, described the final scene as 'the nastiest [*häßlichste*] . . . for which a German stage has ever been used'.[22]

The overwhelmingly negative response to Act Two reveals much about the interplay between prevailing aesthetic standards and the actual process of reception. Rather than considering what point Hauptmann might have been trying to make in foregrounding sexuality, the spectators took offence at the mere fact that he did so.

Thus, the last episode of Act Two demonstrates that Helene's social consciousness has been raised by Loth, as she makes her bold and principled stand on behalf of the unfortunate Marie and against the hypocrisy of her stepmother. The spectators might have considered the positions of the characters involved, and have come either to approve Helene's gesture or to side with Frau Krause; instead many of them reacted only to the subject-matter of the dispute. Explicit reference to characters sleeping with each other was just the sort of obscenity they knew they

could expect from a Naturalist play, and here as elsewhere they resisted looking beyond their immediate sense of repulsion.

Many critics of *Before Sunrise* and of other Naturalist works reproached the writers for dwelling on unpleasant aspects of life – on alcoholism and other illnesses, as on poverty, degradation, and vice. Treating the Naturalists' choice of subject-matter as a reflection of their unnatural preoccupations was a way of refusing to confront the writers' real aims: 'The Naturalists' intentions of criticizing society were thus denounced as a mere joy in wallowing in "filth".'[23]

For the Naturalists, the key criterion was of course not filth, but truth. In the 1880s, the notion that art should aspire to truthfulness was restricted to the mostly young would-be innovators such as Hauptmann and the founders of the Freie Bühne. The dominant conception of drama corresponded rather to the ideas set out by Gustav Freytag in 1863 in a playwriting manual called *The Technique of Drama*, where he wrote:

The most important thing for the poet is the aesthetic effect of his own invention, for the sake of which he plays around with and changes the real facts however it suits him.[24]

That the sequence of events in Act Two of *Before Sunrise* constituted a plausible depiction of life in this setting would therefore have been virtually irrelevant to most of the spectators.

The Court and the Forceps

While the court sanctioned Kastan's first, verbal outburst, they indicted him for the second, purely physical gesture with the forceps. In explaining their opinion of Kastan's disruption of Act Five, the court determined:

He brought what was only being talked about on stage into *actual* view in the auditorium, and in doing so he even outdid what was taking place on the stage and transplanted the offensiveness – if one wishes to regard the events on stage as offensive – right into the auditorium. But this involves crudeness for which the author of the play cannot be held responsible.[25]

The court posits a hierarchy of causes of offence, according to which the discussion of a potentially offensive subject is necessarily less reprehensible than the actual representation of that subject; and a dramatic representation on the stage is less likely to give offence than presentation in the immediate vicinity of the spectators.

Act Two of *Before Sunrise* involves not just discussion but the on-stage representation of drunkenness and of characters who have recently been engaged in sex, and moreover extra-marital sex; therefore, to the court, Kastan was perfectly within his rights in protesting verbally against such a spectacle. But the final act of Hauptmann's play, as it was performed at the premiere – without the moaning of the woman in labour – did not go beyond the first of these three level: that is, beyond the subject being talked about, until Kastan's gesture took the event from the first level to the third, from discussion to enactment in the auditorium. Whereas the court's ruling on Kastan's first interruption implied that they regarded any form of protest as justifiable, their response to his conduct during Act Five suggests that they did not consider all defensive tactics as legitimate.

In this respect, among others, the court's judgement of Kastan's two actions presents some telling inconsistencies, in that several of their objections to the gesture with the forceps might also be raised against the shout of 'Are we in a brothel?' The primary measure applied by the court to determine whether or not the Freie Bühne was justified in expelling Kastan was the extent to which his behaviour had contravened the purpose of the organization. They ruled that Kastan holding up the forceps 'went directly against the purpose of the organization – that is, presenting dramatic performances to other people, because these other people had come to see the play, but not the defendant's forceps'.[26]

The other members of the Freie Bühne did not attend the performance to see Kastan's forceps, but neither did they do so to hear him shout out rhetorical questions. And if holding up the forceps 'transplanted the offensiveness right into the auditorium', did

Kastan's outburst not do the same? The court even maintains that a demonstration such as Kastan's with the forceps could have prevented the performance from continuing; yet why would a gesture incite a riot so much more readily than a shout?

Distinguishing Manner and Matter

One reason for the court's divergent judgement of the two incidents is that, to them, discussion of or allusions to childbirth are not in themselves offensive, whereas references to sexual relations are. Here the court appears rather more open than the majority of the audience. In analyzing the spectators' opposition to the final act of Hauptmann's play, Landau wrote that 'the discussion of matters having to do with the delivery of children . . . was felt to be crude'[27] – an apt formulation, in that the spectators witnessing the performance *felt*, on an instinctive level rather than the rational one on which the members of the court were supposedly operating, that the repeated mention of childbirth was crude.

For the court, the substance of *Before Sunrise* thus warranted Kastan's protest against Act Two, but not his protest against Act Five. However, if the court found talk about childbirth unexceptionable, clearly they felt differently about the sight of a pair of obstetrical forceps. It seems that for the male court, forceps in the theatre constituted 'matter out of place', and one detects beneath that conviction a broader fear of things female entering too openly into the bourgeois public sphere.

Above all, the court was objecting to the manner of Kastan's gesture with the forceps because it failed to function as a clear protest *against* the performance. Both Kastan's disruptive actions were scripted, but whereas 'Are we in a brothel?' sets an alternative text against that being acted out on stage, by holding up the forceps Kastan was, on the face of it not, so much protecting himself against the performance as offering it help. The court condones verbal but not physically enacted self-defence by the members of an independent theatre society; presumably if during the final act Kastan had shouted 'Are we in a delivery room or a theatre?', the court would have declared his actions to be justified throughout.

Overall, the court's response to *Before Sunrise* was somewhat less conservative and more discriminating than that of Kastan and many of the spectators at the premiere. Act Five appears to have offended the majority of the audience just as much as Act Two did. Yet, while the court's decision flatly states that Act Two contains 'disgusting things',[28] it emphasizes that Act Five would give offence only 'if one wishes to regard the events on stage as offensive' – that is, any repugnance depends on the individual's subjective view.

No doubt the men who made up the court agreed with the conventional wisdom that drama should not aim to reproduce reality, but they did distinguish between both different forms of representing reality and different kinds of reality. Of course, they were able to reflect on the issues; the audience reacted largely spontaneously to a performance which repeatedly transgressed their notion of what drama should be.

Implications of Kastan's Victory

Yet the court's task was not to evaluate Hauptmann's play, but to judge Dr. Kastan's conduct. They pronounced Kastan's behaviour innocent in one instance, culpable in the other. That suggests that the contest was tied, but in fact Kastan won on points: the court ruled that, since the law requires 'persistent violation',[29] and the defendant had thus far committed only a single offence, the Freie Bühne was not justified in immediately expelling Kastan.

Having achieved this victory, Kastan chose to withdraw after all, and returned his membership card to the Freie Bühne. This implies that for him there was above all a principle at stake in the case, that of the members' right to express their objections to the works being performed by the new organization. Once his protests against *Before Sunrise* had been vindicated by the court, Kastan presumably felt that the best form of further opposition was to boycott the Freie Bühne by ceasing to patronize its productions. However, he must have come to revise this dismissive view: in a memoir about Berlin published in 1919, Kastan devotes only a few lines to the Freie Bühne, but does express considerable respect for the founders' motivation, declaring 'The non-material impetus of this organization cannot and shall not be disputed, even here.'[30]

Kastan found other means of continuing to express his objections to the Freie Bühne's selection of material. Apparently when the board refunded his membership dues, he declined the money and requested that it be donated instead to an organization for the reform of habitual drinkers.[31] This refusal to accept the money presumably went along with the principled stand Kastan felt he had made throughout the conflict. And by requesting the donation, he again enacted a typical response to Naturalism, implying that the theatre ought not to preoccupy itself with the likes of alcoholics, who would benefit far more from being 'reformed' than from misguided efforts to dignify their wretched lives in works of dramatic art.

In the circular originally sent out by the board of the Freie Bühne announcing the expulsion of Dr. Kastan, they justified their action by the need to 'ensure that everybody in the audience for Freie Bühne theatre performances observes those social proprieties which are customary in the company of educated persons'.[32]

It is ironic that the men who ran this progressive theatre society, whose *raison d'être* was to produce work which fell outside the parameters of current theatrical practice, did not expect their members to react in anything other than the usual and 'proper' manner. They wanted it both ways: freedom to experiment and innovate in their selection of plays, along with freedom from active resistance by the spectators.

There is further irony in the fact that Paul Schlenther, in his book about the reception of *Before Sunrise*, twice describes Dr. Kastan's actions during the premiere as *unanständig* – that is, 'indecent'.[33] He thus criticizes Kastan in the terms frequently applied to Naturalist works by their opponents, invoking a stable boundary between what is acceptable and unacceptable.

Yet the 'social proprieties which are customary' are not stable, but rather currently prevailing, historically determined norms of conduct. In fact, only a few decades earlier, conventional audience behaviour throughout Europe and North America – even in the respectable, establishment theatres – was quite unruly, as it had been for centuries. Not until the latter half of the nineteenth century did audience response in the theatre develop towards the model we nowadays regard as normal, whereby the spectators sit quietly in the dark facing an illuminated stage, and applaud only at conventionally accepted moments and at the end of the performance.

The uproar at the premiere of *Before Sunrise* – like the uproar at, for example, the first production of Alfred Jarry's *Ubu Roi* in Paris in 1896 – constituted a scandal only because by the 1880s and 1890s theatre audiences were no longer expected or 'supposed' to react vocally during a performance. By rebelling against this reduction of theatre spectators' right to self-expression, Dr. Kastan forged a link between himself and the disorderly audiences of the past who regularly protested, especially against new plays.

Conclusion

Dr. Kastan was quite a well-known figure in the cultural life of Berlin, described by one contemporary as 'a character of the most comical sort and a furious enemy of the "new movement".'[34] In keeping with that attitude, Kastan's protests against *Before Sunrise* have usually been depicted as either eccentric or amusing. Yet it would be wrong simply to dismiss Kastan as a reactionary who resisted Naturalism in general and *Before Sunrise* in particular out of a self-serving interest in preserving the status quo of patriarchy and class inequality. All that was no doubt the case: yet it is equally true that he showed greater energy and imagination in protesting against the premiere of *Before Sunrise* than those responsible for the production showed in responding to his actions.

Kastan's spirited resistance to Naturalist theatre of course proved ineffective. The single performance of *Before Sunrise* represented a vital breakthrough for the new movement, and the climate for and nature of theatrical practice in Berlin and beyond were soon transformed. The public's criteria and tastes underwent a gradual yet far-reaching alteration.

Indeed, the fact that the play had been the cause of such widespread controversy and such passionate expressions of support and opposition meant that subsequent, potentially scandalous productions seemed tame by comparison. Playwrights such as Hermann Sudermann found success in the early 1890s with works which, while considerably less strictly Naturalist in theme and composition than *Before Sunrise*, would not even have reached the stage in the previous decade.

With the benefit of hindsight it is possible to argue that the Berlin audience was itself bored with the stale fare being offered by the theatres in the 1880s – that the bourgeoisie was eager to be stimulated by the shock of the new and found Naturalism a welcome change.[35] Close examination of the premiere of *Before Sunrise* reveals signs of this more open-minded attitude even amid all the fervent protests. Those audience members who hushed Kastan during the love scene of Act Four were probably more receptive to new material and approaches than was Kastan, and perhaps more so than they themselves realized.

The importance of the premiere of *Before Sunrise* for German theatre history is well known. The less familiar story of the three-sided encounter between Dr. Kastan, the Freie Bühne, and the Berlin court emblematizes key changes in the history of theatre and audience: Kastan's stunts point backwards to an earlier form of the theatrical event; the court's judgement reflects the transitional nature of the period by endorsing his right to protest, but only with substantial qualification; and the stance of the Freie Bühne points forward to twentieth-century norms of audience behaviour which, perhaps regrettably, remain restrained.

Notes and References

1. Curt Baake, review of *Vor Sonnenaufgang* (Hauptmann), Freie Bühne, Berlin, *Berliner Volksblatt*, 22 Oct. 1889, reprinted in *Berlin – Theater der Jahrhundertwende. Bühnengeschichte der Reichshauptstadt im Spiegel der Kritik (1889-1914)*, ed. Norbert Jaron, Renate Möhrmann, and Hedwig Müller (Tübingen: Niemeyer, 1986), p. 96–7. All translations are my own.

2. Cf. Heinrich and Julius Hart, 'Das "Deutsche Theater" des Herrn L'Arronge', *Kritische Waffengänge*, IV (1882), quoted in Norbert Jaron, Renate Möhrmann, and Hedwig Müller, 'Zur Berliner Theatergeschichte', introduction to Jaron, Möhrmann, and Müller, eds., op. cit., p. 2.

3. Otto Brahm, 'Der Naturalismus und das Theater', in *Kritiken und Essays*, ed. Fritz Martini (Zurich: Artemis, 1964), p. 411.

4. Paul Schlenther, *Wozu der Lärm? Genesis der Freien Bühne* (Berlin: S. Fischer, 1889), p. 22.

5. Julius Bab, *Das Theater der Gegenwart: Geschichte der dramatischen Bühne seit 1870* (Leipzig, 1928), p. 56.

6. Schlenther, op. cit., p. 22.

7. Gerhart Hauptmann, *Vor Sonnenaufgang* (Frankfurt: Ullstein, 1959), p. 32.

8. Adalbert von Hanstein, *Das jüngste Deutschland: zwei Jahrzehnte miterlebter Literaturgeschichte* (Leipzig: Voigtländer, 1901), p. 170.

9. Baake, op. cit., p. 96.

10. Cf. Isidor Landau, review of *Vor Sonnenaufgang* (Hauptmann), Freie Bühne, Berlin, *Berliner Börsen-Courier*, 20 Oct. 1889, reprinted in Jaron, Möhrmann, and Müller, eds., op. cit., p. 90.

11. Schlenther, op. cit., p. 28.

12. Ibid.

13. Regrettably, it is not now known exactly what cuts were decided upon for the production at the Freie Bühne: cf. Gernot Schley, *Die Freie Bühne in Berlin* (Berlin: Haude und Spenersche Verlagsbuchhandlung, 1967), p. 50. But Landau was mistaken in referring to 'the woman giving birth, whom one could definitely hear sighing in her labour pains off stage' (p. 90); Schlenther reported that this was one of the many details in the script which the Freie Bühne chose to cut (p. 28), and the court's decision corroborates his version (p. 134).

14. Max Osborn, *Der Bunte Spiegel: Erinnerungen aus dem Kunst-, Kultur- und Geistesleben der Jahre 1890 bis 1893* (New York: Friedrich Krause, 1945), p. 131.

15. Landau, op. cit., p. 90.

16. Quoted in Peter De Mendelssohn, *S. Fischer und sein Verlag* (Frankfurt: Fischer, 1970), p. 109.

17. 'Der Naturalismus vor Gericht,' *Freie Bühne*, I, No. 5 (Mar. 1890), p. 134.

18. Ibid., p. 133–4.

19. Cf. Baake, op. cit., p. 96.

20. 'Der Naturalismus vor Gericht,' p. 134.

21. Ibid., p. 133.

22. Landau, op. cit., p. 90.

23. Jaron, Möhrmann, and Müller, op. cit., p. 31. This essay has provided me with much useful background information for this article.

24. Gustav Freytag, *Die Technik des Dramas*, tenth ed. (Leipzig: S. Hirzel, 1905), p. 15.

25. 'Der Naturalismus vor Gericht,' p. 134.

26. Ibid.

27. Landau, op. cit., p. 90.

28. 'Der Naturalismus vor Gericht,' p. 133.

29. Ibid., p. 134.

30. J. Kastan, *Berlin wie es war*, second ed. (Berlin: Rudolf Mosse, 1919), p. 265. Kastan also alludes, rather abstrusely, to the role he played in the history of the theatre: 'It is unnecessary to go into details about the life of the Freie Bühne organization, for reasons which are obvious to anyone in the know.'

31. De Mendelssohn, op. cit., p. 110.

32. Ibid., p. 109.

33. Schlenther, op. cit., p. 31, 32.

34. Osborn, op. cit., p. 131.

35. Cf. Jaron, Möhrmann, and Müller, op. cit., p. 35.

Yun Tong Luk

Post-Colonialism and Contemporary Hong Kong Theatre: Two Case Studies

The case of Hong Kong – acquired by the British under treaty, and restored to Chinese sovereignty in what some perceived as merely a shift from colonial to neo-colonial rule – always seemed a special case in the debate over post-colonialism. In NTQ53 (February 1998) Frank Bren looked primarily from an artistic and administrative viewpoint at the connections between film and theatre in the former colony: in the article which follows, Yun Tong Luk explores the social and cultural significance of two influential local productions, staged almost a decade apart – one, *We're Hong Kong*, shortly after the Sino-British Joint Declaration of 1984, the other; *Tales of the Walled City*, coinciding with the moment of Hong Kong's reversion to Chinese rule. He points out the uniqueness of post-colonial experience in the territory, and examines the ambivalent attitudes of the Hong Kong people before and after the change of sovereignty.

IN RESPONSE to the recent proliferation of academic interests in post-colonial studies, *Modern Drama* dedicated its Spring 1995 issue to this topic, covering a wide spectrum of post-colonialities in theatre practice.[1] The subsequent year witnessed Helen Gilbert and Joanne Tompkins's book, *Post-Colonial Drama: Theory, Practice, Politics*, 'the first full-length study to examine how performance practices intersect with and develop an understanding of post-colonial theories'.[2] And in NTQ53 (February 1998) Frank Bren looked at the wider spectrum of performance in Hong Kong, with particular reference to the close connections between film and theatre in the former colony.[3]

In spite of concerns such a fashion for post-colonial theory might have brought in its train,[4] to read literature, drama, and culture with a post-colonial mind-set or in terms of post-colonial theory can prove to be a relevant strategy, since 'the post-colonial covers all the culture affected by the imperial process from the moment of colonization to the present day'.[5] This strategy is of special topical relevance to Hong Kong's cultural productions before and after the hand-over to China on 1 July 1997.

Hong Kong had been under British colonial rule for over a century and a half, and for the ten years prior to its reversion to Chinese sovereignty underwent a process of steady change in the political, social, and cultural spheres. Most of these changes, relating to the eventual reversion to Chinese rule, have been manifested also in art and literature, and in particular the theatre. Neither in its decolonization nor its post-colonization did Hong Kong manifest sudden change, but rather a process that was seen as both gradual and inevitable.

Ever since the signing of the Sino-British Joint Declaration in 1984, Hong Kong theatre has thus been conducting a series of explorations on issues ranging from identity – cultural as well as ethnic – to other aspects of post-colonial existence. Like other post-colonial countries, Hong Kong has exhibited some typical post-colonial characteristics of a regional entity with self-pride, presumed political liberation, economic self-sufficiency, and cultural autonomy. But in its status as a Special Administrative Regional Government within China, it differs from most post-colonial territories in not having achieved independent nationhood, and thereby has distinctive post-colonial characteristics.

Firstly, in the long and arduous process of decolonization, whether ideologically or in practice, Hong Kong has been subdued in its combative or resistant stance toward its colonial master – indeed, the response of

Hong Kong artists to British colonial rule has never been belligerent or violent. While trying through theatre to give some form of identity or consciousness to Hong Kong, the tone of the theatre has been non-combative and even at times reconciliatory, rendering its will to liberty or freedom from colonialism lukewarm and ambivalent.

Secondly, a post-colonial Hong Kong is not equivalent to an independent Hong Kong, British sovereignty being supplanted by reversion to Chinese rule. Viewed from historical, nationalist, and cultural angles, this reversion is a justifiable change, but not necessarily an alleviation of the fears and anxieties of Hong Kong's people. Far from being euphorically hailed as a return to the motherland, at its worst this change of guard may be feared as a transition from imperialism to neo-imperialism under the guise of national unification.

Since the racial and cultural bases of Hong Kong are identical to those of China, issues of separate identity and cultural distinctiveness, so often necessary for a place to assert itself as nation, become irrelevant in the context of Hong Kong, with autonomy from China culturally as well as politically out of the question. From this derives the third factor – the mixed feelings of Hong Kong people towards the new era: euphoric for some, ambivalent for most, even mildly resistant in some quarters. The euphoria was displayed to the world in a façade of fireworks ascending into the night sky of Hong Kong harbour. The ambivalence was, by its nature, less prominent, but surely lurking behind this celebratory canopy. And the resistance was no better demonstrated than by the protests of a handful of ousted democratic legislators on the eve of the hand-over.

These characteristics of the Hong Kong version of post-colonial response have made their presence no less felt in theatrical productions. The periods leading up to and following the transfer of sovereignty have provided aesthetic stimuli to new forms of representation on the Hong Kong stage in terms of productions, dramatic texts, and critical response alike – the first two having more

to do with form and content in Hong Kong's theatrical scene, and the last with a more heightened awareness on the part of the audience.

By looking at these three areas I want to explore some of the theatrical representations of ambivalence and desire and the cultural and ideological indeterminacies thus expressed, and to analyze the demands, theatrical as well as extra-theatrical, which a more identity-sensitive audience will make upon the theatre.

I am taking two representative theatrical productions of the past decade or so as points of departure – both local productions of original texts, and both reflective of the cultural and social zeitgeist. These are *We're Hong Kong* (1985) and *Tales of The Walled City* (1994). To varying extents, both works demonstrate how post-colonialism in Hong Kong is related to the process of cultural production. The post-colonialism of Hong Kong drama and its discourse as reflected in these two productions typify responses to British colonialism in their material, cultural, political, and historical manifestations.[6]

'We're Hong Kong' as Collective History

We're Hong Kong was a bilingual play staged in 1985 by the Sino-British Repertory Company under the artistic direction of the late Bernard Gross, an Australian who had for some years worked in Hong Kong. The script was co-written by Hardy Tsoi and Raymond To, two prominent local theatre workers, and reached the stage just after the signing of the 1984 Sino-British Joint Declaration with regard to the future of the territory on the principle of 'one country, two systems'. This timing could not have been more significant.

The play describes seven local characters, six Chinese and one British, who are in search of their identity in view of the uncertain future of their homeland. In their soul-searchings, the play encapsulates in one hour or so the past history of Hong Kong. Both in content and style, the play lends itself to post-colonial explication and analysis.

As a dramatic text, *We're Hong Kong* does not follow conventional linear development: its narrative is a series of episodic events in fourteen scenes, tracing the collective history and cultural memory of Hong Kong.

One: The Prologue.
Two: The Beginning of Colonialism.
Three: Life by the Sea.
Four: Mutual Benefits.
Five: Post-War Rebuilding.
Six and Seven: Trends of Colonialism.
Eight: Sino-British Talks.
Nine: Emigrant's Blues.
Ten: Moods of a Wanderer.
Eleven: International Student Party.
Twelve: Proper Pronunciation.
Thirteen: Roots of Hong Kong.
Fourteen: The Voice of Hong Kong People.

These fourteen scenes run the gamut of the territory's history, from the 1841 cession of Hong Kong to Britain, through the 1941 Japanese occupation, the gloomy years of the early post-war period, the social unrest and economic boom of the 'sixties, the economic boom of the 'seventies and the bewilderment of Hong Kong overseas students, to the joint Sino-British declaration of 1984, and the subsequent uncertainties that befell the people of Hong Kong.

In terms of stagecraft, the production exploited a variety of techniques ranging from mime, stylization, direct address to the audience, monologue, singing, irony, hybrid usage of both Chinese and English, fluid and free movement of the actors on stage, and the multiple roles they assumed to flaunt the hybridity of the production.

Generically speaking, it is difficult to categorize *We're Hong Kong* in any conventional sense: on the one hand it is a political drama, on the other it is a prime example of a social problem play– yet it also contains, for example, elements of improvisational theatre. The political intention was quite clear, but the questions raised, though familiar, were not sharp or poignant enough to give offence to the colonial authorities. One of its co-writers, Hardy Tsoi, admitted in interview that the content might be provocative but was never meant to be subversive.[7]

The haunting questions the play managed to raise are none the less realistic and pertinent; their representations through stage techniques, variously illusionistic and non-illusionistic, aptly dramatizing two conflicting and complementing cultures at work under colonial rule. The hybrid forms of representation, while adhering to no dominant dramatic form, function within colonizer/colonized circumstances which bear the trademark of post-colonial drama: rather than invoking a binary superior/inferior model, they supplement and reinforce each other, the combination suggesting the unique malleability and flexibility of Hong Kong culture in its post-colonial context.

The Ambivalence of Identity

Of the fourteen scenes, Scene Eleven – the climax of the play, dramatizing the ambivalent feelings of Hong Kong people about their identity, nationalism, and personal freedom – is especially worthy of mention. It is set at a party sponsored by the International Student Union, where the regional participants are all supposed to sing on behalf of their countries. When it is Hong Kong's turn, the students are at a loss: reluctant to sing 'God Save the Queen', neither do they wish to sing the anthem of mainland China. Out of desperation, some choose to sing a pop song, 'Kowloon, Hong Kong', redolent of *The World of Suzie Wong*.

However, in the background, one student suddenly cuts in with a cherished Chinese folk song, 'In a Land Far Away'. This lone voice gradually overwhelms the previous song, culminating for all the students in an emotion-laden moment reflecting the lost generation of Hong Kong, and suggesting that cultural identification rather than political identification is more reassuring and meaningful to their diasporic status.

A similar diasporic identity crisis afflicts the only non-Chinese character in the play. Also the only one who can speak impeccable English, he chooses to see Hong Kong as his home. However, thanks to this very language barrier, he feels both alienated and rootless.

Emblems of cultural imperialism in *We're Hong Kong* (1985).

Yet bilingualism in this play has two meanings – one referring to hybridity of language, the other to the two versions of the script itself. The English version is for the convenience of the expatriate audience, but proved to be a burden to local actors. However, the late artistic director, Bernard Gross, did not think this was the case: to him,

From *Tales of the Walled City* (1994).

speaking English and acting in drama are two different issues, and the linguistic barrier would not undermine the local actors' Chinese identity or status, as against the advantage of drawing more expatriates to participate in local cultural productions.

Initially, the English version was made necessary since the Repertory was invited to perform in English in the 'Come Out' Youth Arts Festival in Adelaide, Australia. But the bilingualism also inadvertently revealed the role changes of the British Council in Hong Kong, since the Sino-British Repertory was founded in 1979 with British Council funding with a view to promoting English studies in local high schools, usually in the form of bringing in British actors to perform in local schools – basically, reinforcing a colonialist education policy.

However, in 1982 the Sino-British Repertory was given a grant by the Hong Kong Development Council of Arts, and subsequently became more independent from the British Council. As drama productions grew increasingly Cantonese-centred, more space and agency were created for post-colonial discourse and critique.

'Walled City' and the China Factor

Ten years after the staging of *We're Hong Kong*, another large-scale production of a post-colonial drama came in the form of a musical, *Tales of the Walled City*. The opening production of the fifteenth Hong Kong Asian Arts Festival in October 1994, this saw an unprecedented joining of forces among the three foremost professional repertories in Hong Kong – the Hong Kong Repertory of Drama, the Hong Kong Chinese Music Orchestra, and the Hong Kong Dance Company – the elements of the spoken drama, singing, and dancing all represented, and sharing equal importance.

Billed as an original musical drama to be given ten performances in October 1994, it played to full houses and was revived in January 1996, playing to eleven full houses. Some modifications, mostly in connection with dancing and musical choreography, were made for the revival in response to criticisms incurred during the first run, but the artistic director, Dr. Daniel Yang, spoke in defence of the original: 'Let those who are critical of our singing and dancing finesse indulge in their notion of what a Broadway musical should be. After all, we are trying to tell a Hong Kong story and represent local life.'[8]

However fair or otherwise one may judge comparisons between this local production and Broadway muscials – and it would seem fair enough for the audience to expect a high quality from the three top professional performing bodies in Hong Kong – the main issue does not lie in technical finesse or professionalism, but rather in the matter of style and audience identification. To damn or defend the production in the shadow of Broadway musicals misses the point: for the style and format of the singing and the choreography evoked more of mainland China than anything Hong Kong audiences would have readily identified from previous experience. Hence, one gets the impression of the mainland upstaging Hong Kong, and

From *Tales of the Walled City.* Top: the defeat of the pirates in the Ch'ing Dynasty. Bottom: outside the Walled City in the 1950s.

the centre – albeit a new centre – marginalizing the local.

While novelty and originality are to be commended and are warranted in an experimental work, this cannot mitigate the fact that the local audience found it hard to empathize with a performance supposedly telling their own story. The local rhythm of heterogeneity, the zeitgeist that marked each important era of post-war Hong Kong, were overwhelmed by the colourations of a mainland style production.

This tendency towards discounting 'the China factor' was understandable in the context of post-colonialism and the imminence of 1997. The second run attempted to tone down the Chinese influence – but in my opinion inadequately when the show came to dealing with the 'fifties and 'sixties in Hong Kong. Traditional Chinese orchestral accompaniment clearly evoked less of the hybrid nature of the era than rock'n'roll and pop music.

The timing of this performance has often been hailed as a post-colonial representation of Hong Kong on the eve of the reversion of sovereignty; and certainly the show offered its own post-colonial critique of Hong Kong's past, present, and future, as of its search for identity and ambivalent relationship with China. The demolition of the old walled city, infamous for its crimes, and its reconstruction as a public park here becomes a metaphor in the narrative, displaying Hong Kong's history from 1841 onwards to the 1990s, underscoring the importance of localism and the values that have made Hong Kong what it is.

Avoided in the process, however, are such sensitive topics as dominance, suppression, and resistance between colonizer and the colonized, the Japanese invasion and occupation of Hong Kong, the Chinese civil war and its influx of refugees, the social unrest of 1967, the aftermath of Tienanmen Square in 1989 – and, amazingly, the confrontation between the inhabitants of the walled city and the authorities. Dominant instead is the theme of co-prosperity between colonizer and colonized in fighting off the pirates and building Hong Kong as a place of abode.

Recalcitrance and resistance are muted in the interests of a politically sensitive production: rather it is full of reconciliatory and celebratory affirmation, of the building of a new Hong Kong predicated on a carnival logic which aims at arousing a more positive collective imaginary for a better future.

Tales of the Walled City is not a realistic dramatic representation but a romancing of the history of Hong Kong, smacking if not of a commissioned at least of an occasioned piece of production, trading on the collective wish-fulfilment of the populace. It is not surprising to hear that a third run for the show is in prospect, at a time when Hong Kong is in process of rebuilding its confidence for the future.

Notes and References

1. *Modern Drama*, XXXIII, No. 1 (Spring 1995).
2. Ann Wilson (in 'Introduction', *Modern Drama*, op. cit.), cites Linda Hutcheon's concern that this fashion 'represents another of the First World academy's covert colonizing strategies of domination over the cultural production of the third world'. See Hutcheon's 'Colonialism and Postcolonial Condition: Complexities Abounding', in *PMLA*, CX, No. 1 (January 1995), p. 9.
3. Frank Bren, 'Connections and Crossovers: Cinema and Theatre in Hong Kong', *New Theatre Quarterly*, XIV, No. 53 (February 1998), p. 63–85.
4. Helen Gilbert and Joanne Tompkins, *Post-Colonial Drama: Theory, Practice, Politics* (London; New York: Routledge, 1996).
5. Bill Ashcroft, et al., *The Empire Writes Back: Theory and Practice in Postcolonial Literatures* (London; New York, 1989), p. 2.
6. These two productions were by no means unprecedented. Other productions by local theatrical companies had antedated them, for example, Zuni Icosahedron's *The Opium Wars: Four Letters to Deng Xiao Ping* (1984) and Hong Kong Repertory's *1841* (1985).
7. 'Zelda Cawthorne Reports on a Hong Kong Play', *South China Morning Post*, 6 July 1985.
8. Daniel S. P. Yang, 'On the Re-run of *Tales of the Walled City*', *Tales of the Walled City*, Urban Council Presentations, No. 1 (1996).

Poh Sim Plowright

The Art of Manora: an Ancient Tale of Feminine Power Preserved in South-East Asian Theatre

When is a widely-known fairy tale more than a story? Poh Sim Plowright recently went to South Thailand and North Malaysia to examine the relevance of the 'birdwoman' folk tale to the lives of the villagers in those two regions. Here the local people still participate in a ritual dramatization of a story which for them represents a crucial renewal of life in their yearly calendar – a celebration of the roots of feminine magical power which goes back to the ancient historical south-east Asian practice by which a victorious ruler would carry back as booty to his kingdom the wives and dancers of the vanquished. Since most of the members of these royal harems were mediums gifted with special powers of healing and communicating with spirits, they were seen as valuable additions to a ruler's aura of divinity – and consequently to his terrestrial power. More importantly, the theatrical art form known as *Manora*, which enshrines the 'birdwoman' tale, is said to have been founded by two royal female trance mediums, regarded as primal healers and guardians of a life-renewing elixir: thus, each performance also serves as a shamanic and healing ritual. The performances here described by Poh Sim Plowright also have links with drama in China and Japan, and at the end of her article she explores the powerful connection with W. B. Yeats's celebrated 'birdwoman' play, *At the Hawk's Well*, which features a 'Hawk' Woman guarding a 'well of miraculous water' against male intrusion. Poh Sim Plowright is Director of the Centre for the Study of Noh Drama and Lecturer in Oriental Drama at Royal Holloway College, University of London.

A hunter sees a beautiful birdwoman bathing in a forest pool; he steals her feather robe and captures her with a noose. The captive is taken by the hunter to his master – a prince – who forces her to be his bride and later to bear his children. While her husband is away on an expedition, she becomes hopelessly enmeshed in a web of court intrigue that threatens her with imminent death. However, she is sufficiently resourceful to recover her stolen feather robe on the pretext of perform-ing a pre-sacrificial dance and this enables her to make her flight to freedom.

STILL SUNG or recited by Japanese fisher-men, Swedish hunters, and North American Indians, the story of the 'birdwoman' con-tinues to cast a world-wide spell, and though it cannot be traced to a single source, there is one place in which this tale of female magic and resourcefulness is still performed as a vital theatrical ritual to large and enthralled, participating audiences. This is the province

of Nakhon Sri Thammarat – in Pali Sanskrit, *Nagara Sri Dhammaraja* or 'The City of the Sacred Dharma King' – in South Thailand. Situated on the old Malay Buddhist site of Ligor, which in the fourteenth century became part of Thailand (known then as Siam), it once shared with the ancient capital Ayuthaya the distinction of being one of the two most powerful cities in south-east Asia.

Until fairly recently, the North Malaysian states of Kedah, Penang, and Kelantan also celebrated the 'birdwoman' story through theatrical performances. But the increasing Islamic antipathy towards theatre[1] has led to an almost total prohibition of performances in Kelantan and only infrequent ones in Kedah and Penang. The mainly Buddhist Nakhon Sri Thammarat is therefore the one place where the power of this story remains undiminished and its theatrical expression officially sanctioned. Here, the heroine of the story, 'Manora' (from the Sanskrit *Manohara*) has given her name (abbreviated to 'Nora'), to the seminal theatrical genre of South Thailand.[2]

Apart from the celebrated story of the birdwoman *Manora* – the captive bride of Prince *Suthon* (from the Sanskrit *Sudhana*) – there are altogether twelve distinct narratives which comprise this theatrical form, which employs a mixture of song, dance, clowning, and skit. In fact it is common in a modern theatrical presentation of *Manora* for the principal story, as outlined above, to be omitted altogether – both a testimony to its deep familiarity in the consciousness of its audiences, and a recognition that its original base must be considerably widened and modernized to include not only other tales from Thai literature but also current popular stories.

Story and History

One of the problems confronting anybody researching the *Manora* theatrical art is the dearth of hard evidence compared to the wealth of anecdote concerning its historical origin, function, relevance, organization, and preservation. Responses to direct questions are invariably oblique or anecdotal, and, though always entertaining, cannot be taken as verification of data from a scientific viewpoint. The problem of documenting *Manora* data is further compounded by the fact that those who are steeped in its tradition – 'The Keeper of the Sacred Crown', for instance – either genuinely cannot dissect it or dare not for fear of breaking its magic spell.

This is, of course, difficult for the western mind, accustomed to sifting material and separating story from history. The truth about *Manora*, which has evolved from a story, is that it is almost impossible to distinguish the historical from the interpretational. In the realm of female trance mediumship in which this theatrical art is sited, fiction and inventiveness are paramount: the female medium in a seance, fulfilling her function as story-teller, magician, and healer, is at her most authoritative, commanding the highest respect from the community through her fictive persona; before she became a medium,

she was usually an ailing individual, of little consequence in the village.

And so 'narrative', by flouting all rules of probability, assumes disproportionate significance in this society – displacing the western reverence for demonstrable data, which is regarded in these communities as alterable by the transforming power of the story. By this token, the strange story of the *Manora* heroine and her capture by a prince can also (as will be shown later) be read as the history of a south-east Asian power struggle which was dominated by the seizure of royal trance-medium wives as booty.

The Tale and the Occult

There is a further dimension to this rare form of drama, one that exerts a strange power over local people and brings it into the world of magic – the term 'Nora magic' even being used to express this power. In Southern Thailand, for example, there is an expression *mi ta sua nora*, which describes a person who has fallen under the charm of *nora*, as well as various superstitions like that of *thuk khru*, which suggests succumbing to the curse of a *Nora* leader. The use of these terms points to the existence of an almost indefinable power, with its roots both in the origin of the universally known 'birdwoman' tale and in the peculiar history, organization, and continuation of the *Manora* theatrical genre, which make it undoubtedly one of the world's most potent and occult dramatic forms.

In Northern Malaysia (which was part of Thailand until the beginning of the present century) the *Manora* form is not only inextricably linked with magic of a general nature, but specifically with 'female' magic. This connection is reinforced by the fact that the Malay word for 'magical power'– *empu* – is itself incorporated in the common term for the female: *perempuan*. There is no doubt, then, that from an etymological viewpoint, and even in a strongly Islamic country where women ostensibly take a secondary place and where the *Manora* art is now officially banned, the 'female' is associated with 'magical power'.

The Two Princesses

If we examine the stories concerning the two legendary founders of the *Manora* theatrical form – the Thai princess *Nuensamli* and the Malay princess *Mesi Mala* – there is a strong link between these two royal females as spirit mediums and practitioners of the art of healing.[3] Their journey from ill health to spirit possession and finally to the role of 'healer' is the archetypal induction of neophyte to shamaness. The Thai princess *Nuensamli* was possessed by a god which led to her insanity and exile. A son was born to her who was taught the art of dance by mythical birdwomen called *kinnari,* a clown was magically created from a rock, and a god became a mortal to play the third character in the genre.

This formula of using three male roles played by actors (the last one 'masked' to undertake more than one part), originated from the *Manora* theatrical art form and has dominated Thai drama as well as later masked theatrical genres in south-east Asia.[4] In the Malay 'Kedah' version, the princess *Mesi Mala*[5] contracted a strange illness as a result of spirit possession which led to an obsession with drumming on a coconut shell – the use of a drum[6] being another characteristic feature of the induction of a shamaness, since the drum is the instrument most conducive to trance possession.

A group of children followed her in this strange occupation, and they were exiled to an island called Pulau Kecang where they were joined by the clown[7] figure, *Phran Bun,* who first appeared as an Indian bead-seller. He returned to India and brought back from the Buddha to the princess the famous 'crown' – a major element in a *Manora* performance. The princess's return and intervention through dance produced the healing which saved her nation from an epidemic, turned the founder into a source of healing, and began the *Manora* theatrical art form.

It is believed that in a performance the spirit of *Mesi Mala* enters the body of a female dancer in trance and reinforces the healing power of this theatrical genre so deeply rooted in female trance mediumship.

Nora Sompong Thombulbana, the 'Keeper of the Sacred Crown' (supposedly brought back from the Buddha) in Nakhron Sri Thammarat.

375

From the literal and figurative perspective, there is perhaps no clearer connection between the rites of female trance mediumship and theatre than those manifested in *Manora:* invocations at the beginning and end of the performance to the original female medium founder, whose presence is visibly attested to by the altered state of the trancer she chooses to enter, serve as a strong framework within which the various stages of the drama unfold. Incense, food, and song-offerings merge with dance and trance-inducing drum-beats to constitute elements at once theatrical and ritualistic. Such is the magical aura surrounding *Manora* in Southern Thailand that non-ritual performances hardly exist.

It is important to realize that the two legendary founders of the *Manora* theatrical art – one Thai, the other Malay and Thai – are more culturally unified than the detail of their separate stories suggests. Nakhon Sri Thammarat (formerly known as Ligor), where the *Manora* theatrical genre still thrives, was once part of the old Malay kingdom comprising the countries of Malaya, Siam, and Indonesia, and I will be using two Malay stories drawn from the *Hikayat* (ancient personal histories written for Malay kings to immortalize their kingship) to illuminate the meaning of *Nora* power.

Magic and Power

There is an unmistakable element of magic associated with the organization and continuation of *Manora* theatrical troupes. *Nora* actors will testify that if they have a relative who has been closely connected with this art, their involvement with it is sealed, and *Nora* leaders have the reputation of being able to draw crowds who will follow their performances from one venue to another, totally spellbound.

In short, a *Nora* leader not only enjoys supreme authority over his or her actors, but manages to hold them to their vocation. In their own village, leaders are regarded as both doctors and magicians (the unofficial term in Thai for a doctor is *maw*, which also means 'magician'), and the *Nora* leader

radiates extraordinary magnetism: physical attractiveness and sexuality seem inseparable from *Nora* magic.

Though *Nora* or 'birdwoman' theatre, combining elements of magic, enchantment, superstition, sexuality, and most importantly healing, is essentially of female derivation, whether we are thinking of the universal 'birdwoman' myth or of its theatrical form, power can be transmitted through the male. The word *Nora* can serve as a title followed by the name of the leader (for example, the currently famous *Nora* Yok, born in 1922, who has been performing *Manora* for over fifty years), and the leader can be either male or female, but must be gifted with charisma, sexuality, and powers of exorcism and healing – like the redoubtable Mrs. Manee Burinkoat, shown opposite.

A male leader is usually reputed to have seductive power over his female spectators, with whom he frequently has affairs, and in the legendary competition for attracting audiences between two former celebrated *Manora* troupe leaders, Nora Wan and Nora Toem (the latter having died in 1970), the defeated rival, Nora Wan, was forced to forfeit wives and daughters to the winner[8] – just as in the ancient south-east Asian power struggle between Siam and Cambodia, which resulted in the sack of Angkor by the Siamese in 1431, many royal Cambodian wives-dancers were forfeited to the Siamese ruler and carried off to Siam as part of the victor's booty.

Apart from being spoils of warfare, royal wives-dancers were prized as valuable spirit mediums through whom the victorious king was able to enhance his own magical powers. Underpinning these practices is the ancient Hindu concept of the ruler as a god-king drawing on female chthonic powers of fertility and magic – a belief so strongly adhered to that it had the weight of dogma in the old Malay world of Indonesia, Siam, and Malaya.

The earliest genealogies of the Melaka[9] kings in Malaya have been traced back to the Hindu Chola invaders of India in the eleventh century. Thus, the first known King of Melaka, Raja Iskanda Shah, claiming

Mrs. Manee Burinkoat, the future leader of a *Nora* troupe, instructing her pupils at a rehearsal.

ancestry from the first Chola ruler of India, established a court system characteristic of Hindu kingdoms in India, and the system by which a ruler was symbolically upheld by characteristics of divinity was eventually adopted by other kings in the Malay Peninsula.[10] Every attempt was made to reinforce the ruler's special access to and protection by supernatural powers, since his subjects were determined to see him as someone specially endowed with magical powers, the king being regarded as the supreme medium through whom his subjects could get in touch with the invisible world.

The ubiquitous belief in the power of unseen spirits to influence human affairs brought into relief the crucial role of female dance trance mediums who had been co-opted into a ruler's harem precisely because of their ability to communicate with spirits and so enhance his magicality. There is no doubt that the capture of the 'birdwoman' (a semi-divine creature) to be the bride of the prince in the classical 'birdwoman' tale was part and parcel of the ancient practice of members of the aristocracy linking themselves to spiritually empowered women whose divinity they could share.[11]

Far from being a spectacular detail, the theft of the birdwoman's feather robe and her capture in a noose (a kind of bottled magic) served as a crucial political stratagem to ensure the future ruler's authority over his people – hence the prince's pursuit of his missing wife when she was forced to fly away in the course of the narrative: the future ruler's authority was dependent on, if not equivalent to, the magicality symbolized by his 'birdwoman' spouse.

The central role of the birdwoman's dance in the story, once she regains her feather robe, elevates her performance to a level closer to shamanic ecstasy than entertainment. It is her ambivalence, simultaneously as super-heroine and shamaness, fictitious and non-fictitious, that gives her a unique strength and attraction, since the dividing line between a real-life seance (which is intrinsically dramatic) and the miraculous narrative world of gods, spirits, and semi-divine flying heroines into which the medium transports his or her audience, is virtually non-existent.

Not every shamaness is necessarily a heroine, or vice versa, but the 'birdwoman' heroine and the shamaness share common attributes, including the 'feather robe' and 'magical flight'.[12] Moreover, the 'narrative' passage of the flight of the 'birdwoman' from the corrupt world of political intrigue into that of the supernatural could easily have been borrowed from an 'actual' seance in which the shaman, as story-teller and healer, charts his or her journey from one realm into another.

The fact that the original narrators of this tale were reputedly women[13] has led to the story being regarded as a piece of propaganda for women's rights. But the ambience surrounding this tale goes far beyond that of politics, and even to call it an allegory about male usurpation of the female's control of her body and reproductive function is an over-simplified reading: both the story and its theatrical genre are entrenched in magic in a way that defies categorization.

So scholarly suggestions that the magical flight of the 'birdwoman' back to her own home illustrates the mating and reproductive patterns of certain migratory birds,[14] or that the circumstances prompting her escape reflect the cruel dilemma of social disorientation suffered by a foreign wife[15] surrounded by her husband's hostile relatives, or that the 'birdwoman' story is simply a *jataka* tale[16] concerning the previous life of Buddha, undervalue its complexity.

According to this last interpretation, the Buddha was supposed to have cited this tale as an illustration of how, even in the past, his wife was won only after great effort.[17] Despite the popularity of this theory, the origin of the Southern Thai *Manora* remains obscure and there is little evidence linking it to Indian sources.[18] It is more likely that the origin of this archaic and universally known story is identifiable with the deepest need of the human psyche to explain the mystery and magic of the female in a way that trans-cends propaganda, allegory, social history, and the polemics of gender.

Indeed it is precisely because the tale is so genuinely perplexing, defying all normal conventions and divisions of time, place, culture, narrator and narration, subject and object, that the androgynous world of the medium, where all such boundaries dissolve, provides the story of the 'birdwoman' with its most plausible setting. Hence the close connection between the strongly mediumistic puppet theatre of Southern Thailand – *Nang Talung* – and *Manora*: both belong to the irrational zone of magic where, in the process of communicating with spirits, the dividing line between human and puppet theatres, puppeteers and puppets, trance mediums and the spirits they are invoking, disappears.

Dance and Kingship

As a corollary to the mediumistic implications underlying the dance of the 'birdwoman', it is important to emphasize the role of dance in the old Malay Hindu kingdom as an intrinsic part of the ritual worship of the god Shiva, widely regarded as the Cosmic Dancer and the King of Actors.[19] So, apart from being visually pleasing and entertaining, these court dances, provided by the sovereign's medium wives, ritually and symbolically aligned him with Shiva and not only reinforced his position as ruler over his people but, most importantly, underscored his invincibility, divinity, and protection by the invisible world.

Kingships in the Malay Peninsula did not begin with the Melaka dynasty established in the fifteenth century, but this period so abounds in records concerning the extraordinary role played by women in controlling and balancing spheres of political dominance at court that it is worth scrutinizing just two examples of these women to see what light they shed on the prevalent 'birdwoman' story so central to the old Malay culture: Tun Kudu and her grand-daughter Tun Fatimah,[20] both referred to by historians as *Seri Kandi* – a class of warrior heroines with extraordinary qualities of leadership similar to those of *Seri Kandi*, the legendary wife of *Arjuna* in the fourth century Hindu epic *Mahabharata* (as also to the Valkyries,[21] the 'birdwoman' warrior figures of Teutonic mythology).

Two Historical 'Birdwoman' Figures

Tun Kudu entered the fierce political arena of the Melaka court in 1446, when Raja Kassim, a half-Tamil prince, murdered his half-brother, ascended the throne, and took her as his wife despite her prior engagement to a warrior. She was a daughter of the House of *Bendahara*, an immensely powerful family who thus provided the 'stranger king' with a much-needed local wife to legitimize his kingship. Though not of royal blood, the *Bendahara* was the King's chief minister and would lead the army in the event of a war.

No sooner had Tun Kudu become royal consort than she became the centre of court intrigue: her father was murdered by the king's evil uncle, Tun Ali, who not only assumed the role of the new *Bendahara* but insisted on having the beautiful Tun Kudu as his wife. Realizing the full extent of Tun Ali's ruthlessness and his power to destroy her beloved Melaka, she yielded to his demands. For that she is referred to in the *Hikayat* as *Bungah Bangsa* ('Flower of the People') as well as *Tibang Negara* ('Pillar of the Country').

Tun Fatimah, the grand-daughter of Tun Kudu, was another charismatic figure who dominated the political scene just before the fall of Melaka to the Portuguese in 1511. Like her grandmother, she belonged to the house of *Bendahara*, but she also enjoyed the reputation of being a skilful warrior; and in 1509, disguised as a male warrior, she participated in a battle to drive out the first group of Portuguese traders from the port of Melaka.

Sultan Mahmud, the last ruler of Melaka who died in 1530, ordered the complete liquidation of the house of *Bendahara*, with the exception of Tun Fatimah whom he forced to be his wife. In 1511 when the Portuguese returned with Alfonso D'Albuquerque, the Sultan was forced to flee to Kampar in Sumatra. In contrast to her husband, who was weak, scandalous, and incompetent,

Tun Fatimah is extolled in the *Hikayat* as a high-spirited warrior whose courage and sacrifice in defending Melaka against her adversaries earned her the title *Semangat Melaka* ('Spirit of Melaka'). Through her children she later extended her power to other parts of the Malay Peninsula. Her remarkable skill as a warrior was both a physical and spiritual asset, distinguishing her as a spiritually empowered female of a high order.

In this connection, a point often glossed over in the West is that there is a spiritual dimension in the East to the deployment of martial arts – which are perceived not only as a means of fighting real enemies but also as a way of opposing the host of invisible spirits inimical to humans. In Chinese theatre, which is also strongly directed at appeasing evil spirits, the flags which a general wears on his shoulders in a similar way represent divisions of both actual and celestial armies engaged in combat against terrestrial and metaphysical enemies.

The connection between the staging of Chinese theatre and trance mediumship is very strong, and the fact that martial arts form the basis of Chinese theatre makes them doubly potent against evil spirits, just as *silat* (the Malay term for martial arts) underlies most forms of Malay theatre, and so turns it into an effective offensive against the invisible world

Female Power In South-East Asia

It is true that there is a difficulty in defining female power in a region like south-east Asia. On the surface, male supremacy is taken for granted, within the larger historical context of ancient male-imposed practices such as chastity belts,[22] footbinding,[23] and vagina tightening – this last still current. Indeed these restrictions on the female were so fearsome – tantamount to mutilations in some instances – that there is an argument for regarding them as male counter-offensives against the presence of a deeply felt and feared female force.[24]

It is certainly true that the real centre of power in the King's court in the old Malay kingdom lay with women like Tun Kudu and Tun Fatimah, the arch-mediators of political influence, delicately preserving the balance of power between the 'House of *Bendahara*' (the wife-giver) and the King (the wife-receiver). For this reason, a certain magical force, not unmixed with sexuality, became associated with the 'female' – outwardly tractable and compliant, but inwardly the focus of control and decision-making. There is a Malay proverb which reflects this 'female' characteristic: 'Follow the way of the *padi* stalk; the more it fills, the more it bends.'

The Obliquity of Female Control

It is interesting in this connection that in a country like Malaysia, in which Islamic laws seem to give advantage to the male on issues concerning divorce, inheritance, and the formulation of public policies, at grass roots level, in *kampongs* (or villages), it is *adat* – an Arabic term covering a wide spectrum of age-old customs, proverbs, and mores – which, expressed obliquely if not figuratively, effectively controls and shapes the flow of everyday life in a village and, by extension, the nation. Such is the compelling force of the rule of *adat*, which lies at the heart of Malay life, that there is a saying, *Biar mati anak, jangan mati adat,* meaning 'Better a child die than *adat* perish.'

So just as the House of *Bendahara* (the wife-giver to the King) assumed a superior role to that of the sovereign through the mediating agency of the queen (bearer of future kings), and so enforced the power of 'woman' at court, similarly *adat*, obliquely and relying on an inextricable network of animism, magic, and superstition (elements inimical to Islam), found a way of incorporating and circumventing an indomitable religion to assert its own brand of poetic truth. The following verse, guided by *adat* and ritually recalled during marriage and other ceremonial events, reveals subtle but strong female control in a supposedly male-oriented country:

When we receive a man as bridegroom
If he is strong, he should be our champion.

If a fool, he will be ordered about
To invite guests distant and collect guests near;
Clever and we'll invite his counsel;
Learned and we'll ask his prayers,
Rich and we'll use his gold;
If lame, he shall rear chicken,
If blind, he shall pound the mortar,
If deaf, he shall fire the salutes,
When you enter a byre, low;
When you enter a goat's pen, bleat,
When you tread the soil of a country and
    live beneath its sky,
Follow the customs of that country.[25]

It may be surprising to many to learn that the majority of divorce cases registered in the *Pejabat Agama Islam*, the 'Religious Department' in Kelantan and Trengganu states, were initiated by women. Polygamous marriages are only common among the wealthy urban or elite rural Malays. And the only divorces which do not invite derision are those which take place when the wife is barren and the husband yearns to have children – but if a menopausal wife is put aside so that her husband can marry another, he is likely to be censured by the community.

Women also exercise a certain degree of prerogative in divorce issues and resort to numerous informal procedures to procure a divorce should the husband prove reluctant. According to the writer Wazir Jahan Karim, Islamic divorce laws are not as discriminatory against the female as imagined,[26] and in everyday *kampong* life women assert their power through sexual prowess – the strong implication being that, as with female magic, female sexuality is more potent than its male counterpart. A typical Malay proverb expresses the derivative nature of male power: 'The strength of man lies in woman.'

However, because such a high premium is placed on female sexuality (or more precisely the ways in which it can be deployed), Karim devotes space in her book to enumerating the measures undertaken by women to maintain their sexual prowess. For example, after childbirth, when vaginal muscles tend to slacken or be damaged, many women apparently resort to traditional tonics and herbs (*jamu* and *majun*), which are believed to have the effect of shrinking the uterus, and stomach and tightening the vagina.[27]

The *bomoh* and his patient in the village of Kemasin. The cloth is used to flail the spirit out of the patient.

Within the time-tested scale of village priorities, the wife's ability to resume active sex with her husband takes precedence even over the care of her new offspring. So, not surprisingly, according to Karim, a woman's ability to participate actively in sex is regarded as a far more vital asset than a good complexion or an alluring figure. Hence the idiomatic Malay expression for wife as well as husband is *lawan* – meaning, literally, 'a sparring partner'.

This helps to bring into focus the unusual emphasis on active female participation in marital sexual relationships in the context of south-east Asian social and domestic mores, customs, and expectations – in other cultures a characteristic often associated rather with a mistress than a wife. And – ironically in such an outwardly modest society – 'wifely' virtues elsewhere upheld, like decorum and thrift, are pointedly excluded. Indeed, if the wife is particularly adept at love-making, she is not simply known as a *lawan*, but a *melawan*, or 'super *lawan*'. The fact that such an emphatic differentiation exists, and has

been transmitted into everyday language, attests to the very real power of women in old and new Malay society.

At first glance it might be difficult to see the heavily-robed women in an Islamic stronghold such as Kota Bharu in Kelantan as the real power-houses of the nation, but as I was able to determine for myself during my visit to North Malaysia in 1997, it is the women who control their husband's pay packets, as well as highly lucrative cottage industries like weaving the intricate fabrics for which Kelantan is renowned.

A Visit to a 'Bomoh'

The 'adatization' of Islam, manifested for example, in the inclusion of Qu'ranic verses in animistic charms and spells,[28] has meant that despite the official ban on all ritualistic theatrical performances, which are often indistinguishable from the propitiation of spirits and acts of exorcism, they have been in a sense legitimized, yet still take place on an unofficial basis.

The ambiguous official attitude towards these performances was clearly revealed when I was planning my field trip to North Malaysia in April 1997 to observe *Nora* performances and healing rituals. Although I went through correct official channels, including the Cultural Section of the Malaysian Embassy in London, to get sanction for my research, it was only on arrival in Kota Bharu that I was told categorically that *Nora* performances and exorcisms were banned.

However, accompanied by the local cultural officer, I was taken fifteen kilometres outside Kota Bharu to the village of Kemasin to witness a healing exorcism undertaken by a shadow puppet-master who also serves as the village *bomoh*, or witch-doctor. This ritual turned turned out to be one of the most im-

pressive theatrical feats I witnessed during my entire field trip: no less than a disguised negotiation with the spirit world, capitalizing on the intrinsically dramatic nature of such engagements. Who indeed can upstage an antagonist endowed with charisma borrowed from another world?

The hut of the *bomoh* was in the vicinity of a cemetery, and he and his patient were awaiting our arrival to begin the exorcism. A small area had been prepared for the ritual, and offerings to the spirit world consisting of fruit, flowers, rice, and a pot of incense sticks were laid beside a huge pail of water. The *bomoh* lit the incense, filling the small room with its aroma, and began his incantations in a low, quiet voice. The sick woman sat in front of him and let down her thick of the *bomoh:* his voice became increasingly strident and urgent as he struck the spirit in the patient in a more violent manner.

There were now two conflicting forces in the room, a visible protagonist and an invisible antagonist, and the two were locked in a fierce negotiation, through the real *silat* (martial art) which was originally used to ward off evil spirits. As the volume of the protagonist's voice rose, he called for a branch of the *semeru* tree which is believed to have special powers over evil spirits, and began to throw rice at the patient, initially gently and then more violently. The *semeru* branch was then used to strike the ground in accompaniment to his voice, which rose to an unbearable pitch of authority.

Grains of rice were flying everywhere, but the two combatants had reached a stalemate. Unperturbed, the *bomoh* resumed stroking the hair of his patient, who had remained slumped and inert throughout the entire operation. The seance had ended, but would continue on another day, and the wife of the *bomoh* assisted the patient to the adjoining bathroom where she had to wash herself with the consecrated water from the pail. In a few minutes she appeared with wet hair, looking more reassured. The *bomoh* seemed confident that he would eventually be able to persuade the spirit afflicting her to leave her in peace.

The next day I met the same *bomoh* and his wife at the Gelangang Seni, which is the cultural centre for tourists in the heart of Kota Bharu. He was wearing western trousers and a batik shirt and swinging his car keys from his long tapering fingers. On the agenda for that afternoon were *silat* displays, spinning top contests, and relaxing games like *chongkla* (a board game involving the use of marbles), presided over by his wife.

The compere began to greet a large group of tourists in various languages, and before I knew what was happening I was pulled onto the stage to try my hand at drumming. This was part of the official drive to promote tourism, but the atmosphere of relaxation was beguiling: only what was shown within this cultural complex had been authorized, but it was difficult to distinguish what was

A *silat* display at the Cultural Centre in Kelantan. The martial art form is meant to have power over evil spirits, but here serves as an entertainment for tourists.

and beautiful hair, which he proceeded to stroke with his immensely long, tapering fingers while continuing his incantations and, with his other hand, transferring fruit and flowers into the pail of water.

Almost imperceptibly, his voice rose a little as sprigs of multi-coloured leaves were added to the water until, using a piece of yellow cloth which had been slung across his shoulder, he began to flail the patient, imperiously commanding the spirit to leave her body. Sitting barely three feet away, I became powerfully aware of the entrance of a strange presence which, though invisible, was palpably registered in the reactions truly traditional theatre from the censored fragments of shadow puppet theatre we were permitted to see.

Political interference – either through strict laws forbidding local residents from being involved in their own theatre, or compelling traditional theatrical troupe leaders to obtain licences two weeks before the staging of their shows – strikes at the heart of a form of theatre that cannot really be governed by 'human' time. Since nearly all traditional theatrical performances are shaman-based, and are consequently staged to prevent an epidemic or in response to cues from the spirit world, they cannot be subjected to the whims of an official with the power to grant or withhold a licence.

As though to forestall any further questions from me about the curious position of the Gelangang Seni in promoting theatre officially banned by the powerful Islamic party in control of Kelantan, I was told that its venue was sited on land owned by the Federal Government, and came directly under the control of the Ministry of Arts, Culture, and Tourism, based in the capital. Such casuistry was beyond me, but I noted with interest that on an evening devoted to a shadow puppet performance, and widely advertised among tourists, the huge open-air auditorium in front of the stage (clearly not built according to strict religious prescriptions) was packed with hundreds of local residents fully absorbed in this ancient form of theatre.

To suit the convenience of tourists, the performance ended well before midnight rather than awaiting the traditional waning of the moon, an old superstition which held that by a process of sympathetic magic evil spirits would then be compelled to leave. But for tourism, such an event would not have been permitted; because of it, the sanctioned or 'sanitized' form seemed a travesty of the original.

'Manora' in Thailand

In Thailand things are very different, and while Malaysian contempt for the malpractices of Thai officials at the border separating the two countries is strong – a contempt which extends to the supposedly lax Thai theatrical administrative regulations – there is the highest respect for the potency of Thai magic and the effectiveness of Thai *Manora* cures. Such is the reputation of Thai *Manora* that even the infrequent performances of that theatre form in Kedah and in Penang are undertaken chiefly by Thai immigrants.

So the *Manora* rehearsal of a troupe under the supervision of their future leader and shamaness, Manee Burinkoat, which I saw at the village of Plaiyuan in Nakhon Sri Thammarat, and its subsequent co-performance with another troupe under a male leader at Tung Yai, became the cornerstone of my impressions of this remarkable art form.

Nakhon Sri Thammarat is relatively untouched by tourism, which meant that the *Nora* performances I saw were not diluted but evolved entirely from the needs of the community. Hardly any English is spoken in Nakhon, and the journey by jeep and foot to Manee's hut, where the rehearsal took place, was fraught with difficulties. With the help of torches, we picked our way along overgrown jungle paths through vast plantations of mangosteen, guava, and mango trees, towards the sound of drumbeats reassuringly distinct against a chorus of insects. Market gardening provides *Nora* actors with their main source of income, since their small government subsidies are barely adequate to meet the increasing costs of their elaborately beaded costumes.

Even though it was only a rehearsal, I was impressed by the care taken over detail: as in a performance, each young dancer, dressed as a bird-maiden, was required to perform a salutation to her teacher, Manee, as a mark of respect for her unquestioned authority. Acrobatic stunts were rigorously rehearsed, and these provided the element of spectacle in a theatrical form which is mediumistic in nature. In a seance, just before a medium returns to normality, he or she usually takes a high leap into the air to underline his or her magical powers, and all acrobatic stunts within *Manora*, apart from being spectacular and entertaining, betoken its mediumistic character, though achieved through several

Above: censorship divorces the locals from their theatre, while welcoming tourists. Below: two dancers dressed to resemble the mythical bird (*nok isi*). Note the extended, backward-bending fingernails.

hours daily of rigorous training under their leader.

An exceptionally strong and powerfully built woman, Manee was indisputably in charge. Coming from a strong *Manora* family, she originally felt trapped and tried to evade her vocation, but her husband's severe illness and his miraculous recovery once she vowed to return to the *Nora* fold confirmed her in the inescapability of her current position. The seventy-eight-year-old leader

Nora Huang Napsipong was there that evening, but only as a shadowy presence, and he reiterated his intention of handing over the leadership to her.

'Manora' Performance: Ritual in Action

The joint *Manora* performances I saw in the village of Tung Yai in April 1997 as part of the Thai New Year celebration of *Songkran* exemplified the centrality of this art form to

the lives of the people of Southern Thailand. A great feast was under way on our arrival, and we were invited to participate in it by a handsome young policeman. Hardly were we seated when a tall and striking figure of indeterminate gender, lavishly dressed in white silk, approached our table and welcomed me. This 'apparition', I assumed, was the male leader of the second troupe performing that evening and, in the capacity of village shaman, had dressed in women's clothes to emphasize the superiority of female magic.

In fact, as my guides informed me, the reality was far more bizarre: this figure was the richest and most successful businessperson in the village, and having married and produced children, had then undergone a sex-change operation, settled his wife and children in another village, and as a 'female' grew in wealth, prosperity, and prestige to become the leading figure in the village. The handsome policeman was her husband.

Watching this phenomenon presiding over that evening's *Nora* performance, like the secular counterpart of an all-powerful shamaness holding an entire village in her sway, I was reminded of the *balian* (priestess-shamaness) and *basir* (asexual priest) among the Ngadju Dyaks of Southern Borneo, who act as intermediaries between humans and the gods. (The term *basir* means impotent, and these asexual priests dress and behave like women.)

There was no doubt that the awe in which this person was held by the villagers was linked to her bisexuality: her ambivalence made her the perfect mediator between this world and the supernatural. And so the question of identity became the perfect prelude to an extraordinary evening devoted to renewing the village's unbreakable covenant with the invisible world of spirits – a rare celebration of dual citizenship.

By ten o'clock almost the entire village was spread out on the grass in front of the stage, which was built strictly according to religious prescriptions about the departure of spirits at the close of a performance and the direction of the sun's rays by day. This evening's *Manora* would be devoted to the original 'birdwoman' story and as a special attraction Manee's four-year-old son would be playing the 'clown'/'hunter', capturing each birdmaiden in turn, while the daughter of the male leader of the second troupe had been given the role of the star 'birdwoman'.

It was only later, after my return to London, that it dawned on me that the use of offspring to play key characters in New Year celebrations was not simply a statement about the regenerative principle in *Manora* but the absolute condition of its continuity: like their parents, these two children would never be able to leave the *Manora* tradition, and would forever be caught in the magic circle of its noose. Like the mythological 'rope' used by the god of force to secure the Japanese sun-goddess Amateratsu, when she emerged from her cave in the famous Japanese restoration myth – which later became the *shimenawa* or 'ritual rope' which demarcated the sacred area for a rite of propitiation – the magical 'noose' in *Manora* is a symbol both of captivity and liberation, the crux of the 'birdwoman' story.

These levels of meaning and participation ran through the whole performance: the young dancers in their bird costumes had been turned into magical beings from another world, in conformity to the law well known to the history of religions, that one becomes what one displays. Wholeheartedly they entered the world of make-believe: 'Let us be fishes swimming in a lake; let us be crabs and various types of shell creature moving on the beach.' The male leader of the second troupe performing that evening, who also served as the principal drummer, played like one possessed – at the same time flirting with his daughter, who even at a tender age had inherited her father's charisma.

The Lotus as Symbol

Some of the twelve traditional basic steps in the dance she and the other birdmaidens performed, which bear the descriptive name of the lotus in its various stages of flowering – the closed bud, the newly-open bud, the half-open flower, the open flower, and the fully-open flower – have a meaning that

Acrobatic stunts being rehearsed for the *Nora* performance at Nakhon Sri Thammarat.

transcends description. These movements constitute part of the cycle of twelve basic steps reflecting the twelve months of the year, and so must be regarded as central to the progression of time and life itself.[29] The sexual nuances were at once explicit and implicit, but such was the nature of a public ritual that nothing which transpired on stage was offensive: indeed, the young dancers exchanged repartee which caused ripples of approval to flow through the audience.

The 'lotus' in south-east Asia is a well known symbol of the female genitalia, and it was clear to me that the stage representations went beyond the simple reproductive imagery of the lotus. (This is regarded as the 'king of flowers' in the East, and I could remember that as a child I was allowed to stay up all night to watch a certain variant of this species turn from a bud into a flower in our living-room.) The young dancers were divulging, through floral images in the context of a public ritual, intimate details of sexual knowledge which they had imbibed

from their elders, and the entire proceedings assumed the character of an initiation rite doubly propitious at New Year. This display of dance, improvisation, song, and badinage represented the transitional milestones in a young girl's journey from pubescence to sexual awakening, from the first sexual encounter to full maturity of experience.

In strong contrast to the situation in other parts of Asia, the process of using the 'lotus' image as a way of underlining the central regenerative motif of the 'birdwoman' story was presented with enormous relish. In the famous Chinese play *The Drunken Concubine*, for example, severe political editing has removed the Chinese birdwoman's association with spring flowers[30] and their regenerative symbolism, and so erased the central meaning of the story, which would have connected her with the Thai *Manora*. This, of course, is in line with the current drive of the Chinese Government to excise all traces of sympathetic magic and to place the play firmly in the realm of entertainment.

Much closer to home, such traces do survive: just south of the Thai–Malaysian border, in territory where *Manora* is officially banned, the ritual ceremony known as *cukur rambut* (shaving the hair),[31] is still observed in *kampongs,* those indomitable strongholds of female power. In this rite an infant is passed from the arms of a nubile young girl to those of a blossoming teenager and finally to a betrothed young woman. Barren women, or those who find it difficult to conceive, compete to carry the infant.

Three vital accessories to this ceremony, linking it with sympathetic magic, are a basket filled with boiled eggs and decorated with fresh flowers and shoots (symbols of fertility), a young coconut filled with juice to contain the infant's hair, which has been snipped off by young women of varying ages and will be floated down a river (symbols of prosperity and wealth), and a tray full of ten-dollar bills folded significantly into the shape of birds (symbols of female shamanism and magical flight) which will be given to every female participant.

Money, Sex, and Ritual

Money was a powerful symbol too in the *Manora* performance I was watching at Tung Yai. It was New Year, a time of renewal and rejuvenation, and various of the spectators had rushed to the stage to reward with cash the young dancers who had so delightfully re-enacted the power of the regenerative principle – money as celebration of female sexuality in a country where a far darker connection is more common – the *Bangkok Post* on 15 April having carried an article about the Friday busloads of Cambodian and Vietnamese girls 'sold' to Thai soldiers on the Surin border for as little as 100–300 *baht* (£1.50–£4.50) a time.

Back in Tung Yai there was no pressure: the dance patterns[32] adopted by the young *Manora* dancers seemed repetitive and interminable, shifting imperceptibly from ritual to entertainment and back until it became impossible to distinguish one from the other. Indeed, this is the hallmark of most southeast Asian shaman-based theatres – a trance-like state being induced in performers by a combination of hypnotic drumming and repetitive rhythmic movement, a state which strongly affected me that night in Tung Yai.

I surfaced when the stage seemed to burst alive with acrobatic feats performed by the young dancers whom I had watched rehearsing in Plaiyuan. But although these acrobatic stunts could stand on their own as pure entertainment, and indeed are used as such in performances presented to tourists in the fashionable hotels south of the border, the strongly ritualistic New Year ambience of this particular *Nora* performance presented a different dimension: no mere displacement of normal laws of gravity, but a journey into the super-normal world of the shaman.

What happens when mere acrobatic skill is separated from ritual had been made clear to me during my visit to China in 1994. Here, the actors in Quanzhou, southern China, told me that the ritual sequence called *xi ma*, or 'washing the horse' (an animal associated with sacrifice and exorcism), which in the past preceded an acrobatic display by the groom, prior to the hero mounting a horse, had been banned soon after the Communist takeover in 1949. The sequence required the groom to purify the stage ritually, brushing and saddling an invisible horse, and was thought to be unnecessarily superstitious. I wondered how long it would be before Nakhon succumbed to similar pressures, whether in the interests of tourism or of religious fundamentalism. For the moment I savoured what could be the last vestiges of a hitherto unspoilt theatrical form.

When the young son of Manee appeared on the scene, wearing the sacred *bai noi* (clown/hunter) mask, he received a special ovation since he was making his first stage appearance. His performance of the famous sequence known as *khlong hong*, or 'noosing the birdwoman', was both self-conscious and affectionate: he went from one whirling dancer to another, caressing each in turn and providing the catalyst required to activate the cycle of nature rather than a violent male intrusion into a company of female bathers.

In a semi-ritualistic performance such as this, the hunter's role would more usually be taken by an adult actor who would be equipped for the part in a nearby clearing in full view of the audience. He would be given twelve articles necessary for survival on his journey, including a noose, bow and arrow, flint, and salt – twelve also being the stipulated number of basic steps in *Manora* dance.

Hunting and Cleansing

Customarily the sequence following this is known as *thaeng khe*, or 'stabbing the crocodile' – a symbolic way of showing that the capture of the female must be counterpointed by the destruction of her adversary. This motif is taken from a well-known Thai folk-tale known either as *Kraithong* ('The hero who slays the crocodile') or *Chalawan*, (the name of the beast itself). A huge papiermâché crocodile is placed on a slightly raised platform and the troupe leader uses one of his sacred *Nora* sticks[33] to strike and break it up in a ritual destruction of male bestiality.

Either because of the extreme youth of Manee's son or the highly celebratory context of New Year *Songkran* festivities, 'the stabbing of the crocodile' was omitted on this occasion. Crocodile or no crocodile, we were back to the initial acquatic scenario of dancers pretending to be fishes in a pool, and the show continued till dawn, ending in the traditional way with the first rays of the rising sun, and so capitalizing through sympathetic magic Nature's promise of a new beginning.

This was particularly significant since this performance, staged as part of the Thai Lunar New Year *Songkran* festival (13–15 April), in which the ritual cleansing by water was doubly auspicious: the regenerative core of the play could not have been better served than by the *Songkran* acquatic rituals ushering in the New Year, and nothing is more eloquent than water to express a sense of baptism, renewal, and purification. In this village's syllogism, 'Woman' is associated with water and the intrinsic rhythms of Nature;[34] she is recognized as the regenerative principle, the Great Mother who is the source of the moisture of life, and, according to Eastern belief, she sometimes assumes the form of a Bird, the ideogram of 'god' or divinity.

So what I had seen on stage was the dramatic equivalent of the flow of this life force, as indiscernible as the flow of sap in the trees around me. This 'birdwoman' story, celebrating regeneration, was the very element of cohesion, binding together into a community all the villagers gathered in front of the stage, and this bonding was endlessly repeated in all southern Thai villages celebrating *Manora* and *Songkran*. The varying details of the story with regard to its location either in a lake or river, or its inclusion or exclusion of the feather robe motif, were here immaterial: what was important was its strong image of a female regenerative force connected to or identifiable with the elixir of life, a prize beyond the reach of the male.

That the female is the legitimate guardian of the immortal fluid is the basic premise built into the unalterable structure of the choreography. One of the twelve basic steps, 'Rahu seizes the moon', is devoted to the fight for the immortal elixir, a reference to the well-known episode in the *Brahmanas* (part of ancient Vedic literature) describing the theft of the elixir which is identified with the moon.[35] The subsequent quest for it was the basis of the age-old conflict between the *Devas* (the gods who are friendly towards mankind) and the *Asuras* (the antagonistic gods).

In accordance with the instructions of *Vishnu* (one of the three main gods in Hindu mythology), the ocean had to be churned for the elixir to emerge with all the other healing herbs and jewels, and, while the two antithetical forces were engaged in this task, the Divine Physician, *Dhanvantari*, arose out of the waters bearing the elixir. Though *Vishnu* was determined that only the gods well disposed toward mankind should drink the immortal fluid, *Rahu*, one of the anti-gods, snatched a drop but was beheaded before he could swallow it.

What is significant about the inclusion of this attempted theft of the 'moon' or the 'elixir of life' (both terms being used interchangeably, as in the Chinese story about the goddess of the moon and the elixir)[36] is the strong emphasis on female victory and the healing, life-prolonging aspect of the *Manora* art.

The Japanese Connection

In discussing the power of the 'birdwoman' story, which, as we have seen, survives in more than one form in southern Thailand and northern Malaysia, it is illuminating to compare the 'birdwoman' legacy in the current repertory of the classical Noh theatre of Japan, where two plays revolve around her – one directly, through *Hagoromo* ('The Feather Robe'), the other indirectly through *Yokihi* (*Yang Kuei Fei*), the famous 'birdwoman' concubine of the resplendent eighth-century Tang Emperor, Ming Huang.[37]

The Japanese Noh style of presentation could not be more different from that of the Thai *Manora* with its warmth, sensuality, and reasonable accessibility. The Noh presentation is a model of restraint and economy, and so devoid of any marked dramatic interest that audience involvement is almost imperceptible. Yet *Hagoromo*, in particular, is one of the most frequently performed Noh plays, and the exceptional beauty of its libretto is greatly admired by Noh connoisseurs.

The 'birdwoman' story here is far more familiar to the Japanese than the anecdotes from *The Tale of Genji* (one of the two great national epics) on which many Noh plays were based. And, even more than *Manora*, *Hagoromo* might be considered a perfect mediumistic play – an excellent example of a monodrama in which all the various threads of the story are drastically reduced and forced through the single needle eye of the narrator's viewpoint.

In this case it is the Angel (a moon goddess) whose feather robe has been stolen by a fisherman, and who is thus prevented from returning to Heaven. This central role is usually taken by the main actor – the *shite* – and his virtually complete dominance of the performance finds a parallel in the solo enactments and dances of shamanistic spirit possession in south-east Asia. As the only 'narrator', the *shite* is the holder of the thread of the narrative, though, in the style peculiar to Noh drama, some of his lines are completed for him by a chorus of six or eight chanters who also comment on the narration, adding a dimension of objectivity. However, there is no question that the *shite is* the sole narrator, actor, and commentator of the narrative, just as a trance medium who is solely in control can speak through several voices.

Holder of the Strings

In Sanskrit drama the narrator is called the *sutradhara* – a term derived from puppetry, meaning the 'holder of the strings of the puppets'. Hence, as with several ancient theatres, including the Chinese, the connection between the human and puppet theatres is very close – particularly so with the Noh, whose founder's seminal treatise on actisng instructs his actors to perceive themselves as puppeteers, controlling the movements of their bodies through imaginary strings tied to the heart.

In large measure this has accounted for the remarkable and concentrated control of the Noh actor, as well as the marked similarity of some of his movements to those of string-controlled puppets. And, above all, this dominating puppet analogy aligns an ancient classical 'human' theatre to the well-attested exorcistic efficacy of puppet performances – while also providing a further parallel with the movements of the *Manora* dancers, whose similarity to puppets is taken for granted in South Thailand by a society which has from time immemorial regarded both these arts as effective means of communicating with the invisible world of spirits.

Dancers must thus move like puppets if they wish to be the receptacles of spirits. Similarly, the strong underlying puppet rationale of Noh drama, which defines both its purpose and strategy of stage movement, also attests to its mediumistic character. The single pine tree on the back panel serves as a spirit conductor; and in the two-act structure of a Noh performance, the first features the spirit disguised as an ordinary mortal, the second shows his or her true manifestation,

The Hawk-Woman from Yeats's play *At the Hawk's Well*, as performed on the Noh stage at Royal Holloway.

while the dance which the main Noh actor performs to bring the play to a conclusion reminds spectators of the original dance of propitiation by the young goddess Uzume, regarded as the first shaman, actress, and dancer of this theatrical genre.

Applying this shamanistic perspective to *Hagoromo*, the 'Angel', played by the *shite*, would be described as the 'middle seat' (the one who goes into trance), and the 'Fisherman' (who steals her robe without which she cannot return to heaven) as the 'front seat' (the questioner). The analogy between trance ritual and theatre continues when the blindfolded 'middle seat' is replaced by the semi-blind *shite*, rendered nearly sightless by his restricted wooden mask.

'At the Hawk's Well'

Hagoromo, perhaps because of its muted form, does not feature prominently in the list of 'birdwoman' stories outside Japan. By far the most celebrated play in the West today to have focused on a 'birdwoman' theme is W. B. Yeats's *At the Hawk's Well* (1916), inspired by Noh drama. As a coda, it would be illuminating to compare it with *Hagoromo* and *Manora*, both of which preceded it by several centuries.

Yeats's dance-drama features a 'Hawk-Woman' who guards a well containing the elixir of life. It re-tells the classic story from *Hagoromo* about an angel (moon goddess) who is nearly prevented from returning to the moon by a male through his theft of her feather robe. Yeats substitutes water for the feather robe, but in essence deals with the same male quest for immortality involving male–female conflict. The theft of the water is merely an alternative way of dramatizing the classic theft of the feather robe – a dangerous encroachment on female territory.

Although Yeats, in his famous introduction[38] to Ezra Pound and Ernest Fenollosa's *Certain Noble Plays of Japan*, referred to *Hagoromo* in conjunction with *At the Hawk's Well*, this connection has been largely overlooked.[39] *Hagoromo* and *Nishikigi*[40] – focusing on shamanism, courtship, and birds' feathers – were two of several Noh plays included in Pound and Fenollosa's anthology, and it is no accident that Yeats, while discussing the context and inspiration for his *At the Hawk's Well*, should have been drawn to them because of their thematic affinities.

It would seem that his 'Hawk-Woman' was conceived in the same mould as that of archetypal female trance mediums like the *Manora* heroine, while Yeats's definition of the essence and beauty of 'Woman' refers directly to her extra-terrestrial dimension, which could only be identified with the resonant image of a bird.

Yeats even opens another of his plays – *The Only Jealousy of Emer* – with the line 'A woman's beauty is like a white frail bird, like a white sea-bird', and there is also ample evidence of his involvement with female trance medium activities in the years before the genesis of *At the Hawk's Well:* he attended seances in Dublin with a non-professional medium called Mrs. Mitchell in April 1913, and about the same time was also consulting mediums in London. There is no doubt that his experiences of seances inspired his poetic activities,[41] and it is easy to understand why Yeats, with his strong predilection for the occult and supernatural, should have been drawn to the ancient Japanese drama, not in the spirit of pale imitation,[42] but as a way of interpreting his own occult struggles.

However, despite the strong mediumistic overtones of Yeats's play, it would be difficult for a modern western audience, without a common belief, to see the connection between art and everyday life.[43] So while *At the Hawk's Well* is refreshingly accessible through its clarity of structure and text, and the way it focuses on and leads up to the conflict between the 'Hawk-Woman' and her two male assailants, the story is largely irrelevant to its western spectators. In South Thailand, on the other hand, while the 'birdwoman' story, as it occurs in a ritualistic *Manora* performance, is fragmentary and barely discernible, the level of audience participation is maximum.

In the ritualistic *Manora* New Year performance which I witnessed in the village of Tung Yai in April 1997, I was seeing something vital to village life: a 'well' from which an entire community had drawn its living water since ancient times. And just as it has always been the function of woman to draw the life-sustaining fluid from the well, so it is the female who still presides over this village – her power being symbolized by the mythical and dramatic image of the 'bird-woman', endlessly regenerative and eternal.

In a region where fact is sometimes indivisible from fiction, and magical reality stronger than everyday logic, the real-life episode of the Tung Yai businessman who 'changed' into a 'woman', married the most eligible local bachelor, and gained control of an entire community, assumed a new meaning for me. As she was driven away from the festivity that evening, the purring sound of her white Cadillac could almost have been that made by fluttering wings. A modern 'birdwoman' still kept us under her spell, and it was the power of her estate, at once real and unreal, which was underwriting the feast and putting in motion once again the story of the 'birdwoman' through the twelve steps of the *Manora* – as relentlessly repetitive and self-validating as the twelve months of the lunar New Year.

The question of her identity no longer vexes me. An answer is not required: as with Parsifal's famous question, 'Where is the Grail?' – which awoke the dying Fisher King and the whole of creation – the art of asking is its own answer, setting in motion the cycle of renewal and regeneration at the outset of the Thai New Year. The 'Birdwoman' remains the most powerful manifestation of an ancient tale which even today takes many forms, and whose image, passing freely between heaven and earth, remains central to notions of female power, the sole guardian of the immortal elixir.

Notes and References

1. All performing arts are considered by Islamic purists and the orthodox as *haram* or 'forbidden'. They do not wish to see any kind of human representation, even if it is highly stylized. So the *wayang kulit* or 'shadow puppet theatre' comes under heavy censorship, despite the fact that it was the Muslim philosopher, Ibn Al-Arabi, who saw the *panggung* (puppet stage) as a mini-cosmos, the lamp as the sun, and the puppeteer as

God. Many orthodox Malayan Muslims regard this as a heresy, and the shadow puppet theatre as something sinful. Other traditional performing arts are similarly mistrusted. Ironically, even though the *Manora* theatrical art form originated in old Malaya, it has never been totally accepted by the Malays because of its supposedly strong Buddhist base. See Ghulam Sarwar Yousof, *Panggung Semar: Aspects of Traditional Malay Theatre* (Petaling Jaya: Tempo Publishing, 1992), p. 175, 183.

2. *Manora* was the earliest form of drama known in Siam, and it was believed to have developed in the twelfth century from village performances connected with Buddhist animistic practice in the old Malay kingdom of Patani (just south of Nakhon Sri Thammarat), which is now part of Thailand. In 1909 the British ceded Nakhon and Patani to Thailand under the Treaty of Bangkok. See *The Cambridge Guide to Asian Theatre*, ed. James Brandon (Cambridge: Cambridge University Press, 1993), p. 234.

3. Cf. the role of these two princesses as healers with that of the Japanese legendary Princess Joruri, who is regarded as the mythical founder of the seventeenth-century *bunraku* puppet theatre initially known as *ningyo* (doll) *joruri* (narrative recitations). The story of the romance between the Princess Joruri and the *Genji* general Yoshitsune was well known. Her lover was taken ill during one of his military expeditions, and she flew to his bedside and miraculously restored him to health.

4. See *The Cambridge Guide to Asian Theatre*, op. cit., p. 23–6.

5. For a fuller account of the *Mesi Mala* myth, see *Panggung Semar*, op. cit., p. 165–8.

6. It is believed that the drum is made out of the wood of the World Tree which provides communication between earth and sky. Through his drumming, the shaman is able to project himself into the vicinity of the World Tree and can fly to the sky. See Mircea Eliade, *Shamanism* (New York: Arkana Press, 1989), p. 168.

7. The 'clown' figure is frequently associated with divinity and healing, not only in *Manora* but other related Malay dance dramas: for example, in the Malay female court dance, *Mak Yong*, women who have been healed by *bomoh* (witch doctor) clowns in turn become the healers in the community. See *The Cambridge Guide to Asian Theatre*, op. cit., p. 195.

8. Henry Ginsburg, 'The *Manora* Dance Drama: an Introduction', *Journal of the Siam Society*, LX, Part 2 (July 1972), p. 174.

9. The strategic position of Melaka (now spelt 'Malacca'), at the narrowest part of the Straits of Malacca, made it the most prosperous trading port in south-east Asia in the fifteenth century. The port was named after the Melaka tree, under which the first refugee king – Raja Iskandar Shah – rested on arrival. Kingships in Malaya did not begin with the Melaka dynasty, since the Malay states of Kedah and Patani were known as early as the sixth century. See Wazir Jahan Karim, *Women and Culture: Between Malay Adat and Islam* (San Francisco; Oxford: Westview Press, 1992), p. 34–8.

10. See Richard Winstedt, 'Indian Influence in the Malay World', *Journal of the Royal Asiatic Society*, Parts 3–4 (1944), p. 188: 'Not many decades ago Perak's Muslim Sultan was still waited upon like a Hindu god, by virgins bare to the waist.'

11. Cf. the legendary history and folklore of China, which abound not only in examples of magical flight but specific instances of linking sovereignty with female divinity. See Mircea Eliade, *Shamanism*, op. cit., p. 448–9.

12. See the section entitled 'Shamanic Affinities', in A. T. Hatto, 'The Swan Maiden: a Folk-Tale of North Eurasian Origin?', *Bulletin of the School of Oriental and African Studies*, University of London, XXIV (1961), p. 341.

13. Ibid., p. 334.

14. Ibid., p. 327.

15. Ibid., p. 333, 343. (The 'foreign' wife was frequently associated with sorcery in archaic societies.)

16. Many folk stories were known as *jataka*, and the term exemplified causal connection which, according to Buddhist philosophy, forms the structure of things: every event in the present is to be explained by facts going farther and farther back in the past. See *New Larousse Encyclopaedia of Mythology* (Twickenham: Hamlyn, 1959), p. 355.

17. See Padmanabh S. Jaini, 'The Story of *Sudhana* and *Manohara*: an Analysis of the Texts of the *Borobudur* Reliefs', *Bulletin of the School of Oriental and African Studies*, XXIX (1966), p. 535.

18. See Hatto, 'The Swan Maiden', op. cit., p. 327.

19. Mohammad Ghouse Nasruddin, *The Malay Dance* (Kuala Lumpur, 1995), p. 2.

20. For a fuller account of the lives of Tun Kudu and Tun Fatimah, see H. Haindan, *Tun Kudu* (Kuala Lumpur: Pustaka Antara, 1967); *Tun Fatimah: Sri Kandi Melaka* (Kuala Lumpur: Syarikat Buku Uni-Text, 1977).

21. The Valkyries in Teutonic mythology were not only able to transform themselves into swan-maidens but played crucial roles in controlling the destinies of warriors. See *New Larousse Encyclopaedia of Mythology*, op. cit., p. 278.

22. See the article on chastity belts by Kee Hua Chee, *The Star*, 29 March 1997, p. 2. This was written in conjunction with the world's first full-scale exhibition on this subject, entitled 'Infidelity: Violation of Family Values', held at the Muzium Negara, Kuala Lumpur, Malaysia. Cf. the ancient western concept of *mundium*, central to early Germanic marriage, which expressed a man's dominion over his wife to the extent that should she compromise his *mundium*, she could be smothered in dung (*Lex Burgundronum*, 34.1). See Edwin Hall, *The Arnoffini Betrothal* (California: University of California Press, 1994), p. 15–16.

23. For a full history of the practice of footbinding, see Howard S. Levy, *The Complete History of the Curious Erotic Custom of Footbinding in China* (New York: Prometheus Books, 1991).

24. The following, from Joseph Campbell, *Primitive Mythology: the Masks of God* (Harmondsworth: Penguin Books, 1976), p. 315, is pertinent: 'There can be no doubt that in the very earliest age of human history, the magical force and wonder of the female was no less a marvel than the universe itself; and this gave to woman a prodigious power, which has been one of the chief concerns of the masculine part of the population to break, control, and employ to its own ends. It is, in fact, most remarkable how many primitive hunting races have the legend of a still more primitive age than their own, in which women were the sole possessors of the magical art.'

25. *Women and Culture*, op. cit., p. 66–7. This translation has been ascribed to Sir Andrew Caldwell, former British Resident of Negri Sembilan in Malaya.

26. Ibid., p. 141–3.

27. Though, understandably, any form of tampering with the vagina is a delicate subject, several of those

I interviewed in North Malaysia and South Thailand maintained that they had a friend or relative who had undergone surgery to tighten her vagina. There is a prevalent belief that the vagina is associated with female sorcery. See R. F. Fortune, *Sorcerers of Dobu* (London, 1932), p. 150 ff., and p. 296, for support of this belief.

28. Wazir Jahan Karim, *Women and Culture*, p. 68. Verses from the *Qur'an* are often appended to charms and spells in the form of opening or closing statements. The following spell for 'capturing' a person's soul begins: *Bismillahi 'al-rahmani' I-rahimi* ('In the name of God, the Merciful and Compassionate').

29. See the author's article on 'The Birdwoman and the Puppet King', *New Theatre Quarterly*, XIII, No. 50 (May 1997). As in China, where there are twenty-four splendid 'birdwoman' figures in the famous *Kai Yuan* Temple in the Fujian province representing the twenty-four divisions of the solar year in the traditional Chinese calendar, the 'birdwoman' in southern Thailand is seen as the 'presider' over time, but in a lunar year which comprises twelve months. So the number twelve is significantly repeated throughout the *Manora* art: there are twelve steps, twelve stories; twelve songs; twelve parts of the 'birdwoman' costume; and twelve compulsory articles which the hunter takes with him on his journey. Mircea Eliade writes, in *The Myth of the Eternal Return* (London; New York: Arkana Press, 1989), p. 52, that 'a periodic regeneration of time presupposes, in more or less explicit form, a new Creation – that is, a repetition of the Cosmogonic act'.

30. See an English translation of this unexpurgated scene (with all the spring flowers and their symbolism intact) in Jo Riley, *The Chinese Theatre and the Actor in Performance* (Cambridge: Cambridge University Press, 1997), p. 239–41.

31. See Karim, *Women and Culture*, p. 211.

32. The dance patterns were either circular or in a figure-of-eight, which is a variation of the circle design: apart from being aesthetically pleasing, the circle symbolizes harmony and continuation while the number eight is associated with shamanism – for example, the eight-legged horse connected with the shamaness/guardian spirit of the Buryat tribe. See Mircea Eliade, *Shamanism*, op. cit., p. 469.

33. The same stick is used as an instrument of healing.

34. See Ian Jeffrey's introduction to *La France: Images of Woman and Ideas of a Nation, 1789–1989* (Uxbridge: Hillingdon Press, 1986), p. 22. Jeffrey refers to the great historian and narrator of France, Jules Michelet, who associated woman with water and nature. So 'the spying on Cézanne's group of female bathers entailed an act of violence, a breaking into the cycle of Nature'.

35. A full account of this episode can be found in *World Mythology*, ed. Roy Willis (London: Simon and Schuster, 1993), p. 71.

36. Chang Ee, the wife of the archer Shen Yi, stole the elixir from her husband, and, while he watched helpless, flew to the moon, which became identified with the immortal fluid. Note the reversal of the theft motif in this Chinese story, where it is the female who steals the elixir from the male. Ibid., p. 95.

37. The traditional Chinese version of the swan-maiden story (dated *circa* eighth century) was translated by Arthur Waley, in *Ballads and Stories from Tun-huang* (London: Allen and Unwin, 1960), p. 149–55.

38. This introduction can be found in Ezra Pound and Ernest Fenollosa, *The Classic Noh Theatre of Japan* (New York: New Directions, 1959), p. 151–63. References to *Hagoromo* and *Nishikigi* are on p. 159, p. 161, and p. 159–60 respectively.

39. The Noh play *Yoro*, which features a spring of miraculous healing water, has been considered a more likely model than *Hagoromo* for *At the Hawk's Well*. See Richard Taylor, 'Assimilation and Accomplishment: Noh Drama and an Unpublished Source for *At the Hawk's Well*', in *Yeats and the Theatre*, ed. Robert O'Driscoll and Lorna Reynolds (Yeats Study Series, Canada, 1975), p. 137–8. A close scrutiny of the context of *Yoro* emphasizes the deep differences between the two plays and, furthermore, Yeats himself made no such connection in his famous essay. It should also be noted that *Hagoromo* is a play strongly associated with the famous Umewaka family, responsible for the transmission of the great Noh art to Yeats through Fenollosa and Pound. In 1970 the Japanese Ministry of Education made a film of a particularly memorable Umewaka performance of *Hagoromo*.

40. In *Nishikigi* the ghost of a woman who rejected her suitor in life is still carrying a piece of cloth called *hosonuno*, which is woven from birds' feathers.

41. See Roy Foster, *W. B. Yeats: a Life. The Apprentice Mage, 1865-1914* (Oxford; New York: Oxford University Press, 1997), p. 453–91.

42. In 1949 a Noh play entitled *Takahime* or *The Hawk Princess* was composed by Mario Yokomichi as a complement to Yeats's Noh-inspired *At the Hawk's Well*, and this is regarded proudly by the Japanese as closer to the genuine Noh form than Yeats's 'imitation'.

43. On 17 October 1996, with financial assistance from two Japanese foundations, two productions were organized on the Noh stage at Royal Holloway, with Umewaka Naohiko, the great-grandson of Umewaka Minoru (who introduced the Noh to Yeats), playing the double roles of the Angel in *Hagoromo* and the Hawk-Woman in *At the Hawk's Well*. This was the first time that such a juxtaposition had been made, and it was appreciated as an apt hymn to the Irish–Japanese connection. But, despite the underlining of strong mediumistic resonances in both plays through the distribution of sprigs of rosemary (a sacred herb) to every spectator, the burning of incense, and other devices, audience involvement in the productions was warm but academic.

NTQ Book Reviews

edited by Maggie Gale

Theatre History to 1900

David Wiles
Tragedy in Athens
Cambridge: Cambridge University Press, 1997.
230 p. £35.00.
ISBN 0-521-6268-1.

This book is concerned with 'spatial practice' and the performance of tragedy in fifth-century Athens. Combining a structuralist approach with insights drawn from Henri Lefebvre's work on the materiality and historicity of space, David Wiles explores how tragedies as performances were 'created within and in response to a network of pre-existent spatial relationships'. Throughout, he criticizes the aesthetic and ideological assumptions that he discerns in Oliver Taplin's work (in particular in *Greek Tragedy in Action*) and that he sees as representing 'a normative position within the academic community *vis-à-vis* Greek tragic performance'. Through this critique he is able to articulate a very different viewpoint, continually 'opening up a gap between "Do I see it?" and "Did they see it?".'

In Chapter One, he explores some attitudes and approaches to space, and argues that the concept of performance can help to connect the tragedies with the Athenian specifics of time and place. Chapter Two, the longest in the book, reviews the evidence for spatial dynamics in the fifth-century Theatre of Dionysos. The next three chapters build on this evidence to examine the actions, dynamics, and theatrical meaning of the chorus, while Chapters Six to Eight explore some important spatial oppositions (left/right, east/west, inside/outside, and upper/lower). Two final chapters investigate, on the one hand, visual icons and sacred versus accessible space, and, on the other, the spatial polarity of performers in the *orchestra* and spectators in the *theatron*.

While rooted in the specifics of fifth-century Athenian culture, Wiles's argument is constantly illuminated by references to twentieth-century productions, from Max Reinhardt to Peter Stein and Nancy Meckler to Ariane Mnouchkine. In its insistence on the concrete and social nature of 'performance space and theatrical meaning', this book should have a broad appeal. David Wiles's enquiries are securely based on past and current scholarly research, towards which the reader is directed by full and judicious footnotes. This is a study which deserves a prominent place on reading lists for all students interested in drama and theatre.

LESLIE DU S. READ

Faye E. Dudden
Women in the American Theatre:
Actresses and Audiences, 1790–1870
New Haven; London: Yale University Press, 1997.
£11.00.
ISBN 0-300-07058-6.

This is a well-illustrated, scholarly, and accessible account of women on the (mostly) nineteenth-century American stage and likely, therefore, to appeal to specialist and non-specialist readers. A major strand of the study is concerned with charting the shift from the actress as 'aural' text to the actress as objectified, 'visual' text. Early nineteenth-century American actresses, Dudden argues, had careers which relied not on physical appearances but on vocal skills. However, she notes a move towards the visual in the 1830s. Her case study of 'Thomas Hamblin and His Women' at the Bowery Theatre in New York offers a detailed analysis of Hamblin's exploitation, both economic and sexual, of his manufactured female stars.

The century's increasing commercialization of theatre and of the female body are signalled in the title of the final chapter: 'The Rise of the Leg Show'. Dudden makes extensive use of theatre biography to trace these capitalist and sexist developments. She has chapters on the actresses Fanny Kemble and Charlotte Cushman, and on the actress-manager Laura Keene.

Dudden looks at Kemble's strategies of self-representation, both on and off the stage, to account for the popularity of this English performer in the American theatre and to understand how she was able to 'cleanse' the reputation of the actress. The chapter on Cushman looks at her appeal to women spectators, while the study of Keene highlights the gender-bias against women in management. Dudden weaves the star biographies back into her study by highlighting the ambiguities and contradictions of their success stories – especially as the stars were unable or unwilling to challenge and to change the conditions for ordinary actresses who had relatively little (or rather no) choice about the commodification of their bodies.

Moreover, citing the segmentation of American theatre in the 1840s and the rise of the 'model artist' shows, Dudden is also able to bring the gradual disempowerment of women spectators into her narrative frame. The case-study style of the volume offers the reader the choice of a cover-to-cover or single chapter read. Theatre historians in quest of additional scholarly detail will not be disappointed by the further research contained in the extensive endnotes.

ELAINE ASTON

Twentieth-Century Theatre

Laurence Senelick
The Chekhov Theatre:
a Century of the Plays in Performance,
Cambridge: Cambridge University Press, 1997.
£55.00.
ISBN 0-521-44075-0.

J. Douglas Clayton, ed.
Chekhov Then and Now:
the Reception of Chekhov in World Culture
New York: Peter Lang, 1997. £33.00.
ISBN 0-8204-3085-4.

Chekhov never thought that his work would succeed outside Russia. In England and else-where, his plays were, at first, rejected like some strange foreign virus, a peculiarly Russian disease. And yet, as Laurence Senelick observes, a funny thing has happened: Chekhov has become an international phenomenon, an icon passed from culture to culture.

The Chekhov Theatre charts the history of the plays in performance, covering almost every key production in Europe and the United States, and especially in Russia. The shadow of Stanislavsky is still hovering over Chekhov – the Moscow Art Theatre productions became for many years the model to follow, surrounding the plays with a plethora of conventions and plunging them into a suffocating fog of *nastroenie* or 'mood'. In Russia today, conversely, every director seems to feel the need to break the Art Theatre mould. At times this seems like directorial egoism, but it also reflects a desire to disrupt the dominant aesthetic and release new meanings from the plays.

As Senelick notes, the English-speaking world has generally been more resistant to radical forms of interpretation; but here, too, in recent pro-ductions such as the Wooster Group's *Brace Up!* (variations on *Three Sisters*), the 'Stanislavsky simulacrum' has been challenged, and the cul-tural baggage that surrounds Chekhov's name has been shaken, stirred, and rearranged in intriguing postmodernist forms.

Senelick's book is more than a simple slice of theatre history: it also reflects more than a

hundred years of social, political, and cultural change, inscribed in different productions, and mirrored through the prism of the plays. In each country the story is different, yet the benefit of a cross-cultural study like this is that it makes clear the connections, the reciprocal influences and exchanges, through time and across continents. Senelick's is an ambitious undertaking and an exhaustive piece of research. Inevitably the cover-age of some productions is sketchy but the book will act as a very useful guide, a rich resource, and a stimulus to further investigations.

Chekhov Then and Now, edited by J. Douglas Clayton, shares a similar theme. It is a collection of articles based on an international conference held in Ottawa in 1994 to examine ways in which Chekhov has been received and interpreted in different countries and contexts. The book begins with essays on theatre productions, including Nick Worrall's persuasive reassessment of Robert Sturua's *Three Sisters* and John Tulloch, Tom Burvill, and Andrew Hood's intriguing decoding of Trevor Griffiths's version of *The Cherry Orchard.* Other topics include Chekhov's influence on writers such as Edward Bond and the trans-formation of Chekhov into different media such as ballet and film. Inevitably, this makes for a smorgasbord of a book, an entertaining mixture of methodologies and viewpoints, reflecting the continuing intercultural debate about a writer who – as Senelick concludes – has never ceased being our contemporary.

DAVID ALLEN

Fiora A. Bassanese
Understanding Luigi Pirandello
Columbia, South Carolina: University of South Carolina Press, 1997. £28.50.
ISBN 1-157-003-081-2.

This book is a contribution to the series 'Under-standing Modern European and Latin American Literature'. Its purpose, the editor James Hardin states, 'is to provide information and judicious literary assessment of the major works in the most competent, readable form'. *Understanding Luigi Pirandello* fulfils this brief. It begins with a succinct biographical-historical introduction to Pirandello and proceeds to analyze his output in the following chapters.

The works are grouped thematically: some of the early novels and essays are presented in 'The Late Mattia Pascal and the Goddess Luck'; early plays in 'Right you Are (If You Think So) and the Crisis of Reality'; later fiction in 'Moscarda's Nose, or the Disintegration of the Individual'; the plays *Henry IV, Diana and Tuda, When One is Somebody,* and *Naked* in 'Henry IV's Sane Mad-ness'; the theatre trilogy in 'The Theater Plays'; *The New Colony, Lazarus,* and *The Mountain Giants* in 'Myths'. The final chapter, 'Other Works', gathers together those aspects of Pirandello's writing – for example, poetry and short stories – which do not quite fit the thematic grouping.

Written as a guide for undergraduate and postgraduate students of literature and the non-academic reader, this book does not aim to address issues specific to the study of theatre: there is no sense of the contribution of particular performances to an understanding of the dramatic text, and little information on the development of theatre in Italy and Europe or analysis of theatrical elements in the plays. However, the author shows a sympathetic understanding of Pirandello's concerns, and some of the analyses, notably those of *The Rules of the Game*, *Henry IV*, *Naked*, and *The Mountain Giants*, are discerningly insightful and read very well indeed.

JENNIFER LORCH

Tom Bishop
From the Left Bank: Reflections on the Modern French Theater and Novel
New York; London: New York University Press, 1997.
ISBN 0-8147-1260-6.

Tom Bishop is widely respected as a professor of French at New York University, where he has taught since 1956, and this volume consists of reprints of many of the articles he has written during that period. It is easy to imagine the temptation one might feel, on retiring from a long and fulfilling university career, to sit down and re-edit a selection of one's earlier articles. But the exercise is not without its dangers. Most articles published in academic journals depend crucially on the critical assumptions dominant at the time of writing.

An article on 'Changing Concepts of Avant-garde in French Theatre' may, for example, have been genuinely informative when it was first published in *The French Review* in 1964, but seems rather thin when read in 1998, because it is now divorced from all the work that has appeared on the subject since. An article on 'Role Playing in Genet's *The Maids*' may have seemed quite new in the 1950s (Bishop gives no date for its original publication) but, read today, it offers no more than one might find in any student essay on the subject.

The result of the method Bishop adopts in this book is to present his work in aspic, cut off from the surrounding critical discourse. He rarely refers to other critics, and there is no bibliography. The resulting book is rather disappointing when set beside the major achievement of Bishop's publishing career, his *Pirandello and the French Theatre*, published in 1960. That book clarified the debt owed by writers such as Giraudoux and Cocteau, Anouilh and Salacrou, to the Italian dramatist, and its findings also made it possible for others to draw further connections between Pirandello's metatheatricality and the experiments of later playwrights: it remains an important contribution to defining the emergence of the twentieth-century avant-garde.

DAVID BRADBY

Jerry Dickey
Sophie Treadwell:
a Research and Production Sourcebook
Westport, Connecticut; London: Greenwood.
£63.50.
ISBN 0-313-29388-0.

This is a welcome addition to the 'Modern Dramatists Research and Production Source-books' series, which already includes volumes on Susan Glaspell, Clare Booth Luce, and Rachel Crothers, as well as Sean O'Casey and Elmer Rice. Jerry Dickey's volume results from his extensive research carried out on Sophie Treadwell's papers housed in Special Collections at the University of Arizona, and is of particular importance because of the lack of research so far carried out on Treadwell's work, as compared to that of her contemporaries like Glaspell and Crothers. Dickey's overview chapter, 'Life and Career', gives a full and sympathetic account of Treadwell, still best known for her controversial play *Machinal,* and raises important questions about the ways in which we perceive theatrical/literary careers.

Treadwell is presented as a jobbing journalist and foreign correspondent, and we are given a strong sense of her achievements as an intellectual and social commentator outside as well as inside the theatre. The 'Summaries and Critical Overviews' section is detailed and clearly presented, and will be of much use to scholars and undergraduates alike. Equally useful is the 'Primary Bibliography', which gives insight into the critical reception of lesser-known plays such as *Hope for a Harvest* and *For Saxophone,* as well as her non-fiction writing.

Jerry Dickey points out that Treadwell's life and career were filled with 'unresolved tensions', but that this of course should not detract from the significance of her achievements. Dickey must be given full credit for the manner in which he foregrounds Treadwell's innovative qualities and her 'highly personal theatrical vision', and his volume offers much to those interested in early twentieth-century American theatre in general as well as those with a specific interest in Treadwell and other women playwrights of her era.

MAGGIE GALE

Graham Roberts
The Last Soviet Avant-Garde
Cambridge: Cambridge University Press, 1997.
274 p. £40.00.
ISBN 0-521-48283-6.

This book reveals perhaps for the first time the significance and achievement of a number of writers more or less closely connected with the OBERIU group centered in Leningrad in the late 1920s and the 1930s. It focuses primarily on the work of Daniil Kharms, Alexander Vvedensky, and Konstantin Vaginov, managing to persuade the reader that these ill-fated writers made a genuine contribution to the restless creative experimentation which typified the first decade of this century.

Situated as they are somewhere between their contemporaries the French surrealists and the later absurdists, the importance of the group has long been neglected. This was due at least in part to the fact that Kharms and Vvedensky were both (not surprisingly, in view of their writings) victims of the Stalinist terror, while Vaginov died young in 1934. Yet, as Theatre de Complicite have demonstrated, the work of Kharms at least has proven theatrical potential, and his play *Elizaveta Bam* (available in *Incidences*, translated by Neil Cornwell, and published by Serpent's Tail) might well repay a more respectful revival than Complicite aimed for.

Vvedensky's drama is perhaps even more intriguing, and both *Minin and Pozharsky*, a dialogue of the dead, and the brilliant and fascinating *Christmas at the Ivanovs*, are plays of considerable interest which foreshadow especially the more challenging of Ionesco's drama. Vaginov seems to have written no plays, yet the analyses here shows him to have been a third stimulating, hitherto almost unknown, writer.

The book sets the work in its historical, cultural and political contexts, so that the apparent nonsense and absurdities sometimes acquire a frightening resonance. Roberts's serious and intellectually probing approach uncovers a tiny treasure-trove of modernism, the long neglect of which is clearly regrettable.

ROBERT LEACH

Nicole Boireau, ed.
Drama on Drama: Dimensions of Theatricality on the Contemporary British Stage
Basingstoke: Macmillan, 1997.
ISBN 0-312-16541-2.

This collection of essays begins from the observation that much contemporary British theatre takes for its subject-matter a conscious reflection upon the medium of drama and its operation. In the editor's words, contemporary drama 'can be seen as one long continuous text echoing the changing geometry of twentieth-century culture, a new fractal architecture'. And that's about the sum of it: a potentially interesting idea over-elaborately wrapped up, with a fair quota of buzz-words. And it is never really clear whom these buzz-words are for: many academics will find it dull, many students inscrutable.

For the collection is not really coherent, with some essays having a distinct whiff of the bottom drawer. Casually, a British academic may like to observe what interests the mainly non-British authors – noting the focus on written drama texts, the author canon that privileges Caryl Churchill and Howard Barker, and the method of analysis that is so often description of form and/or content. An exception to this last is Ann Wilson's piece on ghosts and realism in Churchill's work, and even that pulls its punches. But it's a long way ahead of some of the essays.

One author, interested in identifying Christopher Hampton's specific contribution to the contemporary London stage, concludes that he 'sets new standards by making emotional relationships in modern Britain' the subject of a play. A-ha: very 'fractal'. But that's unfair. Such language has by now vanished from the book – thus John Elsom on the final page can nostalgically retrieve creativity from a time 'before the Structuralists dispatched the term to a pre-Saussurean limbo'. Within the geometry of twentieth-century culture, this book is a flat plane: very flat, very plain.

SIMON SHEPHERD

Diane Lynn Moroff
Fornes: Theater in the Present Tense
Ann Arbor: University of Michigan Press, 1996.
£27.95.
ISBN 0-742-10726-7.

This book is one of only two existing full-length profiles, both published in 1996, on Maria Irene Fornes's drama. Moroff's study tries to rectify Fornes's thirty years of marginalization by making her work more accessible on a less theoretical level to a broader constituency of theatre students. Besides contextualizing Fornes's opus within her career and its reception by academics and journalists, Moroff offers an exhaustive analysis of Fornes's five best-known plays: *Fefu and her Friends, Mud, Sarita, The Conduct of Life*, and *What of the Night*. She sets out to analyze the plays as performance texts whose visual images take precedence over their dialogue, arguing that the interplay of theatrical elements enables Fornes to create lyrical plays that explore the power dynamics between people.

For this reason, Fornes's plays resist definitive meanings and instead leave the spectator to sort out each play's multiple perspectives, which exist simultaneously because of the dialectic between text and image. In particular, Moroff asserts that Fornes, using spectacle, constructs and calls attention to female gender roles as seen through mundane activities like stringing beans or ironing. She also argues that Fornes's work is self-consciously metatheatrical, thereby suggesting that the characters on stage serve to question their own role as theatrical devices, in the same way that spectators are expected to contemplate their participation in the theatrical act.

Though some of Moroff's interpretations are debatable, her descriptive analysis of Fornes's dramaturgical structure grapples with the nature of the image in theatre. In this way the book is also a good introduction to how playwrights create images and what effect these images have on the spectators' responses.

STEPHEN DI BENEDETTO

Performance, Theory, General Studies

Peggy Phelan
Mourning Sex: Performing Public Memories
London and New York: Routledge, 1997. £12.99.
ISBN 0-415-14758-X.

I value this book much more for its sudden flashes of insight than for any of its seven main chapters as a whole, which comprise a 'parade of psychoanalytic case histories' in staged collision, dialogue, or mutual haemorrhage with moments of psychic and/or physical trauma in contemporary western culture – such as the crossings of sexual harassment and racism at the heart of the Anita Hill–Clarence Thomas hearings, or Tom Joslin's autobiographical film of his dying from AIDS. These, and ruminations on topics as varied as perspective painting and interiority, the woman dancer's choreographed body, archeological excavation and anality, and the economies of hysterical and narcissistic identifications between white academic women, are delivered through an ostentatious blend of academic essay, fiction, and ventriloquism.

Each chapter is focused on one body part, and explores a palimpsest of loss set up in the Introduction. At the centre is death and its rehearsal, which Phelan identifies with performance as 'the enactment of invocation and disappearance . . . precisely the drama of corporeality itself'. Perhaps loss is 'hard-wired' in the brain to prepare us for its actuality? More locally, both the broader cultural 'making' that sexual liberation seemed to promise, and our trust in words to take us 'to places whose topography we could never map' have died a death.

In order to help reassess 'our relations to mourning, grief, and loss', Phelan essays 'performative writing'. Composed in the context of queer, a subject non-position dead to the symbolic order and liable to repeated rebirth and self-refashioning, it is 'a piece of theatre' inhabiting its own present tense, designed 'to enact the affective force of the event again' by opening itself as any other social performance to 'the psychic process of distortion'. This, rather than 'the restored illustration', might bring us 'closer to the bodies we want still to touch'.

Phelan's 'record of what is and is not possible within the genre of critical commentary' tries 'to forge a different formal relationship between critical thinker and reader', and gestures towards 'a more imaginatively generous way of conducting critical enquiries'. She fears that 'by soliciting the phantasmic so openly . . . I have perhaps lost a certain authority as authentic scribe'. Yet her negotiated brief licenses incontinent word-play, spurts of uncanny coincidence which construct a sense of depth, of access to a realm of the only-faintly-known, which does not so much rhyme with the irrecoverable and mapless body – or with death and its rehearsals, or sororal love as Other to the masculine Imaginary – as with scholarly erudition.

Undoubtedly a work of love wrought out of pain, the book also marks itself, through the homely closures of coincidence and synthesis, as a special gift. In spite of herself, then, Phelan demonstrates that belle-lettrism is not dead. It would be great if, in her next book, she risked losing more. As with Phelan's *Unmarked*, this book has much to recommend it to postgraduate students in any of the arts or social sciences.

MICK WALLIS

Sharon E. Friedler and Susan B. Glazer, eds.
Dancing Female: Lives and Issues of Women in Contemporary Dance
Netherlands: Harwood, 1997.
ISBN 9-05702-026-2.

Dance is a truly embodied art form, and, due to the rise of feminist theories concerning the body, issues of gender have become the predominant theme in dance writing and academic discussion surrounding dance. *Dancing Female* is a collection of twenty-five articles written between 1989 and 1997 which all address in some way the lives and issues of women in contemporary dance. The editors control the structure (subdividing the book into two halves and eight parts) so as to present the complexity of women's involvement in dance whilst building up a picture of a strong female heritage and examining how the relationship between the female dancing body and social meaning has been constructed over the six generations of modern dance. The book covers a wide range of topics and, although carefully and thoughtfully edited with well-written prefixes to chapters, is possibly best enjoyed as one of those books which one can dip into at will, briefly scanning back and forth to place the essay in context if you so wish. What is most refreshing is that the editors give equal status and air space to educators, administrators, and writers as they do to dancers and choreographers, acknowledging the importance of all these roles in nurturing the art form.

Whilst it would be impossible to consider every essay in this review, in the main the contributors' written styles are eloquent, containing some well-developed arguments drawing upon a century of dance criticism. A highlight is Carolyn McConnell's essay, 'The Body Never Lies', an intensely heart-felt philosophical debate with her own experience of moving as a woman. Others I found less satisfying, such as Billie Kirpich's 'Dance Has Many Ages', which promised much but gave little, almost abandoning its debate once the 'thirties were past, and depressingly apportioning the rest of one's life as 'mid-life', worthy of only seventeen lines.

Unfortunately for the British audience, this book has its roots firmly in American dance history and experience, with the exception of Part Eight which presents images of women in particular cultures. Nevertheless the issues under discussion are pertinent to all involved in dance and gender issues, and will be of special interest to dance teachers, students, choreographers and dancers.

HEATHER RUTLAND

Lillian Schlissel, ed.
Three Plays by Mae West
London: Nick Hern Books, 1997. 246 p. £12.99.
ISBN 1-85459-336-6

Ongoing critical interest in the life and works of Mae West cannot afford to ignore the arrival of this fascinating and revealing publication. The playtexts of *Sex* (1926), *The Drag* (1927), and *The Pleasure Man* (1928), all produced on the New York stage, are printed here for the first time. Schlissel's introduction combines biography, a survey of the plays' stage histories, and the criminal prosecutions for infringement of decency laws in the cases of *Sex* and *The Pleasure Man*. The icing on the cake is 'The Case Against Mae West', transcripts of legal documents relating to these prosecutions.

Recent studies, particularly in women's theatre, have revealed the importance of questioning the accepted paradigms for investigating theatre history. The career of West, as revealed here, similarly demonstrates that her work cannot be understood in 'fixed' period terms, but requires placing in a specific social, cultural, and theatrical context. For example, *The Drag* and *The Pleasure Man*, the 'gay plays' (the former is even subtitled 'A Homosexual Comedy in Three Acts'), not only provided work for gay actors, but drew their success from an increasing fascination with gay sub-culture. *Three Plays by Mae West* clearly anticipates a more dedicated critical study into this radical figure of 1920s New York theatre. Meanwhile, Schlissel is to be congratulated for the two decades of assiduity which made this volume possible.

JOHN DEENEY